map to success. It combines
ission – all things I believe in

D0372323

"An inspiring book of global propo....ons, Career Mapping goes far beyond writing a résumé and pounding the streets. It's a book that gives people tools and insights to empower themselves and to make conscious, constructive choices throughout their lives. Get ready for a great lesson in the real world; a lesson I wish I'd had early in my career."
~ GARY E. MCCULLOUGH, CEO CAREER EDUCATION CORPORATION

"As my father John H. Johnson said, 'To succeed, one must be creative and persistent.' I am adding that you must also know how to map your career with Ginny Clarke as your guide. This is a life-changing book!"
~ LINDA JOHNSON RICE, CHAIRMAN, JOHNSON PUBLISHING COMPANY, PUBLISHERS OF *EBONY* AND *JET* MAGAZINES.

"Truly inspiring! This is a GPS that helps you plot a course to success based upon your own unique journey markers. In Career Mapping, Ginny Clarke takes the mystery and the complexity out of overwhelming career decisions. She helps you to be proactive and in doing so gain the confidence that comes from clarity about your motivators as well as your goals and aspirations. This is one of those books you'll keep close to the desk in your home office and read and re-read over the course of your journey."
~ BRIDGETTE HELLER, PRESIDENT, MERCK CONSUMER CARE

"I found *Career Mapping* to be utterly authentic and rich with insight and detail. It offers the reader much more than facts and figures or war stories listing the "Do's and Don'ts" of career building. Instead, this book offers advice in the context of our lives and not separate from our lives. We are not our careers. We are not our jobs or our work. We are not our maps. We are people and when it comes to finding our way in life, Ginny lets us know that we have the power to create it. She shares aspects of her own remarkable life and career that are gifts to anyone who opens these pages."
~ NAT IRVIN, II, THE W.M. STRICKLER EXECUTIVE IN RESIDENCE AND PROFESSOR OF MANAGEMENT, UNIVERSITY OF LOUISVILLE, COLLEGE OF BUSINESS

"Great leaders make conscious decisions about their careers. Ginny Clarke has created the new go-to career guide for everyone from college students to CEOs."
~ SUSAN LUCIA ANNUNZIO, PRESIDENT & CEO, CENTER FOR HIGH PERFORMANCE; AUTHOR, *CONTAGIOUS SUCCESS*, *ELEADERSHIP* AND *COMMUNI-CODING.*

"No matter the age and stage of your career, Career Mapping will help reposition you for the next big thing. Ginny Clarke gives valuable and specific insights for the new college grad to the old school Boomer executive. If you don't know where you are going next, you need a career map!"
~ JOHN E. KOBARA, AUTHOR, A*DOPTING THE MENTORING AND NETWORKING LIFESTYLE*

"A must-read for every woman in the workplace and man, for that matter! This watershed career management book deserves a place on your desk. You'll want to revisit it again and again no matter where you are in your journey."
~ GAIL EVANS, AUTHOR, *PLAY LIKE A MAN, WIN LIKE A WOMAN* AND *SHE WINS, YOU WIN*

Career Mapping
Charting Your Course in the New World of Work
By Ginny Clarke and Echo Garrett

1.Job Search 2. Career Management 3. Career Coaching
4. Employment 5. Career Mapping 6. Executive Coaching

Some names and details have been changed to honor client confidentiality.

Visit our website at MyCareerMapping.com

ISBN# 9781600379901 PB
ISBN# 9781600379918 EB
Library of Congress Control Number: 2011925027
Published by:

Morgan James Publishing
The Entrepreneurial Publisher
5 Penn Plaza, 23rd Floor
New York City, New York 10001
(212) 655-5470 Office
(516) 908-4496 Fax
www.MorganJamesPublishing.com

Edited by Jesse Conrad
Design and Production by
Birkdesign Inc., Chicago
eBook Design and Development by
Birkdesign Inc.
Cover Photograph by Powell
Photography, Inc., Chicago

DEDICATION

HE WHO KNOWS NOT,
AND KNOWS NOT THAT HE KNOWS NOT,
IS A FOOL – SHUN HIM.
HE WHO KNOWS NOT,
AND KNOWS THAT HE KNOWS NOT,
IS A CHILD – TEACH HIM.
HE WHO KNOWS,
AND KNOWS NOT THAT HE KNOWS,
IS ASLEEP – WAKE HIM.
HE WHO KNOWS,
AND KNOWS THAT HE KNOWS,
IS WISE – FOLLOW HIM.
~ PERSIAN PROVERB

TABLE OF CONTENTS

FOREWORD

WHAT GINNY CLARKE DOES IN THIS BOOK IS SOMETHING THAT FEW HAVE BEEN ABLE TO ACCOMPLISH IN THIS ECONOMY— PROVIDE HOPE. Hope for those looking for a job or just wanting to make a change, but too afraid to try. Hope for employers overwhelmed by the sheer volume of applicants and scarcity of matches for the jobs that they are trying to fill. And, hope for policymakers, desperate for ways to accelerate and streamline the process of matching the unemployed with prospective employers. There is literally something for everyone, young and old, working or not, in the pages that follow. Her expertise is in the fast-paced world of executive recruitment, but her wisdom and insights into today's job market are universal, even if you no longer feel relevant in this economy.

Ginny will open your eyes to the reality of today's workplace, help you understand what it means to be truly a free agent, and let you know what employers really want from their employees –for them to be energized by what they do and whom they work for. Passion and perseverance go a lot further in boosting productivity growth than leveraging capital alone. Everyone loses if you hate your job. She will help you make the best of that difficult situation. If that doesn't work, she will help you shift gears, cut your losses, and move on. Yes, even in this economy. Maybe the corporate world isn't where you belong, and a non-profit or a smaller company—even your own—would be a better match for you skills. Not easy, mind you, just better.

A guide, a counselor, and an inspiration is what Ginny is to everyone in her orbit. She can help you to find the path that is only yours to follow. The words are hers, but the work and the results are all yours. She will help you overcome your fears, face your demons, and move beyond the walls of your own insecurities. She will help you prioritize and focus on what you really want from your job, and more broadly, your life. She had me volunteering for a position I felt was out of my reach by the end of Chapter 1!

She is honest and direct, and won't let you remain a victim of your own excuses. There are no shortcuts to proving who you are, and sometimes working hard isn't enough. You need to know your own brand - be willing to step out of your comfort zone and actually assess how you are perceived. This is a difficult but necessary part of the process. Yes, what you wear and how you carry yourself matter. But wearing a great suit and being polished aren't enough if the person inside isn't true to who she or he is. Others will not only see the deception but, also resent you for it.

Ginny is last but by no means least, genuine. She lives and breathes what she writes. She is a force of nature and a way maker, opening doors that few (if any) knew existed. She is also a very dear friend, and after reading this book, I have found even more reasons to love her. She will pick you up, dust you off, and help you clear the hurdles that lie ahead. She will quite simply help you discover an even better version of yourself, which we all could use a little help doing. So turn the page, take Ginny's hand, and uncover the path that was yours to discover all along.

Diane Swonk, Chief Economist and Senior Managing Director, Office of the Chairman, Economic Analysis, Mesirow Financial
··

PREFACE

This book has been long in coming. It started in 2003 as a recounting of my professional and personal journey I hoped would assist others in creating a more purposeful version of their own. It has grown into a methodology and a guide that could not have emerged without the insight, support, and exploration with and from so many beloved friends and family.

My son, Julian Clarke Mowatt, is the light of my life and my greatest inspiration. I could not be more grateful for and proud of the bright, compassionate, creative and determined man you are becoming, Julian. I have learned so much about myself and others by being your mother – the best job I have ever had!

My parents, Elizabeth Campbell Clarke (d. 1997) and Jack Byron Clarke, Sr. (d. 1993) were the best parents my brother and I could have asked for. They were wise and humble; they had a joy for life and a commitment to serve others. They taught me and my brother the power to make our own choices and live with them. To Jack, my brother, who taught me how to get up after having the wind knocked out of me (remember the Judo throw in the front yard?). It is a lesson that has come in handy – metaphorically, thankfully.

My parents demonstrated a true, loving partnership I have found with Thomas D. McElroy II, my precious husband. Thank you, Thomas, for swooping into my life and lighting an eternal candle of joy, unconditional love, and support that I had not known until you came.

Echo Montgomery Garrett has been a Godsend. Her journalistic abilities have brought this book to life. Together we became better authors than either of us could have been alone. Thank you, for your patience, guidance, and skill, Echo.

My spiritual awakening came after my father's passing, and it was sparked by Kurt Hill, Sr. of Holistic Health Practice in 1994. Kurt is a masseuse, healer, scholar, Renaissance man and one of my best friends. Thank you, Kurt, for helping me see and accept so many previously undiscovered aspects of myself.

There are countless friends, colleagues, and coaching clients I am grateful for. You know who you are; you have been there for me cheering me on, questioning my logic, and making me scream with laughter. You feed my soul and you are loved more than you know.

Chicago, 2010

INTRODUCTION

ACCORDING TO WIKIPEDIA, *CARTOGRAPHY*, FROM THE GREEK *CHARTIS* (MAP) AND *GRAPHEIN* (WRITE), IS THE STUDY AND PRACTICE OF MAKING MAPS, OR MAPPING. "COMBINING SCIENCE, AESTHETICS, AND TECHNIQUE, CARTOGRAPHY BUILDS ON THE PREMISE THAT REALITY CAN BE MODELED IN WAYS THAT COMMUNICATE SPATIAL INFORMATION EFFECTIVELY."

NEVER TRAVEL WITHOUT A MAP

The greatest danger for most of us is not that we aim too high and we miss it, but we aim too low and reach it. ~ Michelangelo

Geographically mobile and technologically connected, people are on the move all over the globe. College-educated workers don't stay in one place anymore, toiling at the same corporation for their entire careers. I wrote *Career Mapping* because each move requires courage and specific knowledge if we are to land on our feet ready to charge ahead.

Anytime we are navigating unfamiliar territory, it is natural to feel anxious—especially if there is no map, no directions to follow. All journeys are about discovery, but it helps to have an experienced guide who has been there before. Having been a top-level executive recruiter for one of the world's largest executive search firms, I can shine a light on your choices and prepare you for what you will encounter on your way to the new world of work.

Career Mapping is a guide for finding your dream job straight out of college or for making a career move—whether the move is to a higher rent district or to a different block in the same neighborhood. Think of it as your personal Global Positioning System (GPS) with an unobstructed line of sight to your destination.

I've developed a specific process that enables you to create your own unique career map. (A template can be found at the end of the book.) Whether you are entering the job market for the first time or you're a chief executive officer contemplating your next move, using this career map will help you sort out your options and give you confidence that you are heading in the right direction. You can refer to *Career Mapping* again and again as you move through the stages of your career. Just as pilots are constantly correcting for various factors en route to their destinations, small adjustments in response to feedback and stimuli are in order if you hope to touch down safely where you intended.

Career Mapping draws on your strengths and provides key insights that crack the code of how to be successful on your own terms. It's a code you already have, though you may not know it. If you are willing to do the hard but rewarding work of self-discovery that I guide you through in this book, then—like the hundreds of executives I have placed in top-level jobs—you will be rewarded.

There are no shortcuts. You must assess your starting point and be willing to read the signs and decode aspects of your past—as well as establish targets for your future—in order to create your own unique career map. This guide will point you to a life filled with meaning and purpose that only you can design.

To address all of the levels of career mapping, I have created five different categories of job seekers and career changers to track:

Entry Level

Graduates of high school, undergraduate, or graduate and professional programs. If employed, titles might be trainee, associate, assistant, etc.

Mid-Level

People who have been promoted from an organization's entry level. This role typically involves oversight of and responsibility for direct reports. Common titles are "manager," "supervisor," "associate director," etc.

Executive Level

This level is usually characterized by one's ability to participate in a specific compensation scheme involving pension vesting, purchasing shares or units of company stock, and/or other accumulating assets and compensatory perquisites (or "perks"). Common titles include "director," "vice president," "partner," "principal," "managing director," etc.

Encore Level

Typically a person who is approaching retirement age (age 55 or older), regardless of station or level. He or she might be seeking to stay active and competitive in the workforce, or may be looking to move out of a traditional role and into another area of interest or passion, either compensated or as a volunteer.

Detour Route

This person is challenged by having been out of the job market for a year or more due to a layoff, downsizing, or a personal need like child-rearing or an illness. He or she could be returning from a sabbatical, from running a family business, or from military service that took him or her off course. This person might be starting a business after having held a more traditional job or may be looking for a traditional job after having been self-employed for some time.

No matter which level you are on, moving ahead involves asking the right questions. As you think about where you are now and where you want to go, you will recall key moments that shifted how you thought about your life and your work that brought you to this place. *Career Mapping* provides context for inquiry and examines the wrong questions as well as the right ones.

One journey, many paths, unique career maps. Ready for take-off? Buckle up!

"When once you have tasted flight, you will always walk the earth with your eyes turned skyward; for there you have been and there you will always be." ~ Leonardo da Vinci

Early in my career in banking, I did good work and made my presence felt, but I didn't always have purposeful ambition. As I observed the people who were being groomed for senior positions, the standards for behavior—specifically conformity—became clear. Mind you, people had talent—at least most of them. Some people had more determination, connections, and unbridled ambition than others. Most had above-average intelligence, a strong work ethic, loyalty, and a tacit belief in the mission of the organization.

I was almost always the sole woman and/or person of color in the room. I didn't want to call unfavorable attention to myself. But as a 6'1" African-American woman, I invariably stood out. At a few companies I worked for, I felt merely tolerated. Some of this was my own insecurity about being different. Some of it was my latent resentment about the expectation that I would assimilate, which did not allow me to remain authentic.

From time to time I did succumb and take on expected roles and projects—like diversity—where I had a level of knowledge and understanding others did not. I quickly learned that some of the areas to which I was assigned were undervalued, even marginalized in organizations. Gradually it dawned on me that the characteristics I valued most in myself—keen self-awareness, compassion, and service—were rarely explicitly rewarded in the male-dominated field I was in.

The contrarian streak in me kicked in. I entered another male-dominated arena: the rough-and-tumble world of commercial real estate. I became the third African American hired at Jones Lang

LaSalle (formerly LaSalle Partners), a prestigious firm that had a reputation for quality and exclusivity.

No matter what time zone I was in, my father called me every Sunday morning at precisely 9 a.m. local time. A superintendent (a.k.a. warden) at the California Youth Authority in Southern California, my father had the skills and sensibilities of a CEO, but he was born in an era when those kinds of opportunities were scarcely available to African Americans. My dad—a fair, tough-minded man—served as my mentor and my coach.

When I was 12 and taking an active interest in boys, I brought my report card to my father. He frowned and then chided me for purposely getting A's and B's rather than the straight A's I was capable of earning. He said, *"Don't ever dumb yourself down to be accepted."* At the time, I thought, How did he know? From that point on, I held fast to that lesson.

My parents always challenged me to aim high. Their strong commitment to our community reinforced in me the value of service to others. They also modeled a strong work ethic for my brother and me while maintaining a good work-life balance.

Although my parents were of modest means, they sacrificed to expand my brother's and my horizons by exposing us to everything from sailing and horseback riding to a full range of academic and artistic pursuits. They encouraged us to discover, develop, and play to our respective strengths. Most importantly, they made it safe for us to try anything, make mistakes, and fail—as long as we tried to learn the lesson. In other words, they taught us to believe in a world of possibilities.

My parents also stressed the importance of education. After getting my undergraduate degree in French and linguistics at the University of California at Davis, I left sunny California for cold and windy Chicago, where I earned my M.B.A. in accounting and finance from the Kellogg School of Management at Northwestern University. I looked forward to my Sunday morning calls with Dad; though wide-ranging, the conversation usually turned to my career progress and exchanges with clients, colleagues, and bosses. One Sunday I expressed my restlessness with my current duties at LaSalle Partners.

"Ginny, tell people what you want," my father said. "Be crystal clear. Don't expect them to read your mind."

The next week I spoke to my boss and told him I wanted to be considered for a move to a new position. Within four months I landed the assignment, which was much more interesting than my previous role at the company. In my new capacity I traveled around the country monitoring a portfolio of office and industrial properties owned by a large pension fund. I met people from competing firms whom I can still call friends today.

However, after 18 months in my new position, it became clear to me that my new supervisor was not supportive. I had been reporting to him for two months before he bothered to meet with me—despite numerous efforts on my part to set up a meeting. My supervisor hadn't requested that I join his team; his boss had placed me there, and rather than meet with me on a regular basis, my supervisor assigned a direct report to monitor my daily activities. I had been with the company for four years, and while I was not at risk, I wanted to consider finding a more supportive work environment.

I was soon hired by Prudential Real Estate Investors, a firm which didn't have the same kind of prestige attached to its name, but which did have a long history of profitability and scale. LaSalle Partners managed many of Prudential's properties, and I networked my way to an interview with a senior Prudential executive. In the real estate investment division of Prudential I found opportunity. This division of the behemoth company was restructuring itself to be more competitive in the asset management world, seeking to manage the real estate assets of large pension funds and other institutional investors, in addition to its own real estate assets. I settled in at Prudential and in my personal life. In 1993 I had been married less than a year when I got a devastating call from my mom: Dad had suffered a stroke.

My mother was a physical therapist who met my father when she moved to San Francisco from Tuskegee, Alabama. She came by her fierce independence naturally. Her father, the son of a former slave, walked from Georgia to Alabama to study under George Washington Carver and later became his protégé. Thomas M. Campbell Hall, on Tuskegee University's campus, is named after my grandfather. His middle son, William, was one of the famed Tuskegee Airmen during World War II, making him one of the nation's first black Airmen. In 1948, spurred by their service, President Harry Truman enacted Executive Order 9981, which instituted equality of treatment and opportunity for all persons in the armed services without regard to race, color, religion, or national origin. This order helped bring about the end of racial segregation in the military.

My father's stroke took my mother's best friend. An elegant, active woman, she berated herself for somehow not being able to use her professional training to nurse my dad back to health. A month later, a second stroke took his faculties, and he passed soon after. At that point in my life, his passing was the most gut-wrenching moment I had experienced.

After he died, I stumbled across a file in my father's desk. In it were yellow legal pads filled with detailed notes he'd kept on our Sunday morning conversations. I felt like I'd found a treasure. I was fascinated to see my career mapped out in my father's careful handwriting. He had always urged me to question my course of action and hold myself accountable for the answers. It was never about pleasing him.

Now I called into question what I was doing in my career. The Chicago real estate market hit bottom that year during one of the country's worst real estate recessions. I wasn't sure whether I wanted to stay in the industry. I questioned my spirituality. And although my new husband supported me as best he could in my grief, I secretly began to question the marriage—especially when I measured it against that of my parents. Despite having similar academic pedigrees and social exposure, my husband and I had had very different upbringings that shaped our views of the world in different ways.

These differences in worldview caused competition and increasing tension in our relationship.

Who else gets me? I wondered as I sifted through the evidence that my father had invested so much thought and care into my life and career. Who indeed? I could hear my father's words encouraging me to get all A's instead of coasting with A's and B's. He taught me what I was capable of doing. Could I be the one to best understand the road my father had helped map for me?

Over the next several months, using his notes as a basis, I took a deep dive into my own life and started charting a new course. To my joy, I learned that I was pregnant. As for my career, I decided I wanted to try the field of executive search. After college I had worked in recruitment at the University of California and at Kellogg. I worked in the admissions office and was a member of the admissions committee that interviewed many potential M.B.A. candidates. When I examined my interests, recruitment was a recurring theme.

I knew that the transition into a new industry would be challenging. Top-level executive recruiting was another male-dominated industry—almost exclusively white male, to boot—but that didn't faze me. I was determined to break in. After more than 30 interviews with a leading executive search firm, during which I met with partners in Chicago, New York, London, Copenhagen, and Zurich, the firm declined to extend a job offer.

I felt I was owed an explanation. *"Your experience is just different from what we're looking for,"* came the vague reply.

Couldn't you have figured that out after the first 10 interviews? I thought to myself.

When I was six months into my pregnancy, my brother called with the news that our mother, age 74, had terminal lung cancer. She had smoked 20 years earlier but had quit. In addition to being a physical therapist, she had a master's degree in physical education and remained health conscious throughout her life, swimming several times a week and eating a healthy diet. I prayed that she would live to see her first grandchild born. She did indeed, and she was able to come to Chicago after Julian was born, which was a special time for us.

After my six-week postpartum checkup, in the summer of 1996, the doctor gave me the go-ahead to resume normal activities. Eager to lose the baby weight, I put on my Rollerblades and headed for the park near Lake Michigan, where a tree's root cracking through the asphalt sent me tumbling. I broke my leg just above the ankle and had to be in a cast for four weeks. My mother, who had just returned home to California, came back and helped care for Julian. She later got to see him take his first steps, and I was grateful for that.

Meanwhile, I forged ahead with my plan to take a different career path. I went through 12 interviews with Spencer Stuart, one of the largest global executive search firms, over the course of six months. When I started my job there in 1997, I was one of three African-American women in the global firm. In our Chicago office I was the only African-American consultant and the only female consultant with a child. On June 10, 1997, less than five weeks after my start date with Spencer Stuart, my mother passed.

Again my husband was noble and helpful through all of this heartache, but it became clear that our marriage was not working. We both adored our son, but our love for Julian was not enough to remedy our incompatibility. I felt drained by our union while my young child energized me. My mother saw my unhappiness before she died and said, *"I hate to think of you raising this baby alone, Ginny, but if anyone can do it, you can."*

Six months after my mother passed, I told my husband I wanted a divorce. I had been with Spencer Stuart seven months, I had an 18-month-old son, and both of my parents had recently died. I'm at a big firm where you eat what you kill, I thought to myself. I had never felt more overwhelmed.

After my mother's death, and while I was going through the divorce, I experienced my darkest days. I had no family nearby. Few of my girlfriends had children. And yet I was hopeful. Why? Because I'd been following the map, the clues I found in my father's desk drawer.

All I knew was a fierce protectiveness for my son and a determination to give him the same kind of supportive environment in which

I had grown up: I would maintain a home and an outlook that would allow us both to achieve our highest potential. I took comfort in following the process that I'd begun to rough out in my mind—a map that would take me where I wanted to go and allow me to grow and develop along the way.

Once, during an interview for an opportunity to work with a different group at Spencer Stuart, the interviewer looked at my résumé and said, "*Wow, you've had a meandering career.*"

Excuse me? I couldn't disagree more. What he did not see was that each job and position was a bridge for my varied talents, skills, and interests, and I refused to let his mistaken impression deter me. Why limit myself to land when I knew I could fly?

In the course of my 12 years at Spencer Stuart, and as one of the founding partners and the leader of its global diversity practice, I met, interviewed, and coached hundreds of people. I have used these encounters to formalize the career mapping process, which I use frequently with candidates, friends, and family. My process works. Now I want to share it with you.

In these pages I've noted what works and what doesn't when you're searching for your first job, deciding on a career, seeking a promotion or new position, re-entering the job market after time off, launching a new venture, or creating a post-retirement occupation. That said, there are few absolutes; this journey is of your making, so create it, own it. I offer you a straightforward, practical, and holistic roadmap for every stage of your career.

Recently, reviewing my own career map led me to leave my secure position as an executive recruiter and to launch a talent and career management consulting firm that includes services for employers and executive and career coaching for individuals.

Your own journey will lead to valuable insights that serve as landmarks on your way to a new level of job satisfaction and career accomplishments. Relax and enjoy the process of discovery. I am an experienced guide, and I won't ask you to do anything I haven't tried myself.

MAPPING YOUR COURSE

"TWENTY YEARS FROM NOW YOU WILL BE MORE DISAPPOINTED BY THE THINGS THAT YOU DIDN'T DO THAN BY THE ONES YOU DID DO. SO THROW OFF THE BOWLINES. SAIL AWAY FROM THE SAFE HARBOR. CATCH THE TRADE WINDS IN YOUR SAILS. EXPLORE. DREAM. DISCOVER." ~ MARK TWAIN

1

THE UNCHARTED WATERS OF FREE AGENCY IN THE NEW WORK WORLD

"Let your mind start a journey through a strange new world. Leave all thoughts of the world you knew before. Let your soul take you where you long to be... Close your eyes, let your spirit start to soar, and you'll live as you've never lived before."
~ Erich Fromm

The world of work has changed forever. Not only have jobs been lost, many will never return—at least not in the same form we are used to. Forty percent of the U.S. workforce is predicted to be independent contractors by 2019, up from 26% today, according to Joanne Sujansky, author of *Keeping the Millennials*.

The construct of conventional employment is becoming passé as many companies are choosing—or are being forced to choose, in many cases—to take on independent contractors instead of benefit-laden employees. Some are even rehiring their laid-off employees as consultants or contractors. Employers are crafting creative and cost-effective ways for their workers to manage their careers and lives. These efforts take the form of workweeks that are less than 40 hours, telecommuting, job sharing, and lateral moves.

According to the Bureau of Labor Statistics (2009), people spend an average of 4.1 years at a job and have 7-10 jobs in the course of their lives. This number is up from 4-7 jobs five years ago. Since the best defense is a great offense, you'd best have a map, a strategy to guide you through this journey of inevitable job and career changes.

It is a common perception that one's career path will lead to a single "dream job," but in reality that "dream job" is largely an anachronism. Most people I know have a vision of what the pinnacle of their career climb looks like, but you'll find that you are actually climbing a mountain range with peaks of varying heights. On each climb you'll use different technical skills, and with each peak you conquer you'll be rewarded with a different view of the horizon beyond.

This cataclysmic shift in the new world of work has huge implications for how you manage your career. First and foremost, it means you have to adopt a free-agency mentality. Just like professional athletes, you have to know what your transportable skills are, what you are worth, which teams you would consider playing for, and which factors will trigger a "trade." The difference from the sports analogy is that in the world of work you are representing yourself without the counsel of a high-powered agent.

Having the mindset of a free agent gives you a huge advantage whether you are employed, unemployed, a consultant, or a small business owner. You are the captain of your ship. You cannot be pulled off course because you have your bearings, you know the value of your assets, and you are willing to create opportunities for yourself.

Years ago, during healthier economic times, a friend called to tell me that his position as a real estate portfolio manager had been eliminated. As an executive recruiter, I was used to calls like this, but John wasn't asking me to keep him in mind for new opportunities. He said, "There are three companies I've been tracking and would want to work for. I know people at two of the three, and I know you know the CEO of the third. Will you introduce me to him?"

I did know the CEO; in fact, he had been a friend for years and a client for whom I had done search work. John and I had worked for the same company several years earlier, and I was more than happy to make this introduction. Not only did I hold John's professional capabilities in high regard, I admired his forethought in considering other prospective employers while he was still employed and his ability to effectively leverage his network. I introduced him to my friend and former client, and in short order he received an offer from the firm, as well as an offer from one of the other three companies he targeted. I helped John analyze both offers, and he took the second offer, but he stays in touch with my friend, the CEO to whom I introduced him. This story occurred 10 years ago, and John was my prototype of a free agent. Now, in the new world of work, the free-agency model is more relevant than ever.

Free agents drive change within their organizations in addition to adapting to some of the current workplace and economic conditions. More employees are asking their employers for flexibility to meet familial obligations. Job seekers are choosing companies that honor their social and environmental values. Even with fewer traditional jobs, workers are exercising choice. We are redefining how we work—on our terms. If it sounds like a luxury we can't afford, it is not. It is a paradigm shift whose time has come.

I am not suggesting anarchy, disloyalty, or a sense of entitlement. What I am suggesting is the convergence of workers asking for what they need to be productive, stimulated, and satisfied and employers knowing that they need "optimized employees" to build profitable, innovative, constantly evolving, and sustainable organizations. Talent management in countless organizations all over the world has become increasingly sophisticated, and companies are turning out recruitment, career development, and work-life programs and policies to get the most out of their employees. The timing of this development couldn't be better, since free agents—that's you—are emerging to take control of their respective careers; however, it is important to keep in mind that this self-directed, free-agency approach to career management requires introspection, discipline, and decisiveness.

| Inside Passage

Introspection means reflecting on your fears, values, and passions to guide you in making conscious choices. I've noticed that the hardest thing for many people I have coached or worked with over the years is to grapple with who they are at the core of their beings. It is so much easier to sit passively on the shore and "wait to see what's out there"; easier to simply drift along doing what you are doing; easier just to be buffeted by the waves in this rough economy; easier to stay stuck in survival mode. You can trot out any number of excuses—or you can sit down and begin to plot your own course.

The inability to acknowledge and seek to improve all aspects of what makes you *you* is a common failing. An unwillingness to examine yourself will keep you safely anchored in the harbor and prevent you from the grand adventure of seeking the work and personal life you want and deserve.

There. I said it. I'm asking you to journey through your inner space, a landscape populated by aspirations and dreams, as well as insecurities and fears. Only when you're willing to invest in such a fantastic voyage do you signal to the universe that you find yourself worthy of what it is you say you want. If you limit yourself to staying safely on the shore, you'll never know what buried treasures you might have discovered just beyond the horizon.

Once you embark on your own personal journey of inner exploration, you never arrive at a final destination. It's an ongoing voyage. This inner journey hastens you along the route that you're meant to take.

In my own life I have spent considerable time reflecting on who I am and what matters to me. I can and have performed many roles, and I was better suited for some than for others. I tested myself in several industries and worked for some excellent companies, learning valuable skills, meeting amazing people, and traveling far and wide.

But, in the privacy of my own thoughts, I've had to come to terms with a restlessness that emerged—a longing to speak out, a desire to share my wisdom and help other people find their way. Not everyone takes such a seemingly circuitous path, and I have loved the routes I've explored along my journey. Now I am grateful to have amassed the insights that inspired me to sail into my next career phase armed with courage, conviction, and purpose.

| Preparing for the Journey

Before you set off on a long journey, you must make preparations, and that takes discipline and an investment of your time and consideration. In the case of designing your career map, this involves regularly and systematically doing an assessment of your skills, networking strategically, and researching various aspects of companies and industries.

When you are getting ready for a dream vacation, there's nothing passive about your approach to that trip. You don't just hope to stumble across the perfect itinerary or to pack the right attire. If you want to make the most of your trip, you make plans. You do research and get recommendations. You check the weather. You make reservations. You are proactive.

You also can be frantically busy and scattered in a million directions and fool yourself into thinking you're accomplishing something in advance of your big trip. And yet, when you arrive, you realize you packed all the wrong clothes, forgot to confirm your hotel reservation, and left your guidebook at home. In other words, your dream vacation turns into a nightmare—all because you neglected to take a disciplined approach to planning.

Too many of us take that same haphazard approach to our careers. Let me go back to my friend John. He exercised discipline by looking at possible new opportunities when he was still in good standing at his job. He was prepared to make a move when the time came. How? He made learning a priority. He constantly attended conferences and seminars and set up meetings—not only to serve his clients, but also to learn about other companies and industry trends. He refined the art of strategic networking by striving always to leave a favorable impression. He asked for the help he needed, always showed gratitude, and reciprocated others' generous acts.

| Deciding on a Course

I can't tell you how many people come to me to ask about their job-hunting or career strategies. I invariably ask them which two or three things (functions or roles) they have decided to explore. Eight times out of ten they will talk in vague terms about two or three "jobs that are out there." They avoid naming any specific roles or companies they might approach proactively. When I question this lack of decisive direction and ask if they've thought about specific roles or companies that they might approach proactively, the consistent answer is: "Yeah, I'll think about that if these other jobs that are out there don't work out."

Well, let me let you in on a secret: Those jobs that are "out there" rarely work out, and when they do, it is usually because the applicant was decisive, focused, and proactive in seeking the position.

What gets in the way of exercising our power of choice, that decision-making muscle? Perhaps your parents never let you decide on anything, from what you ate and wore to which college you attended. Maybe they always questioned your choices when you did make them for yourself, causing you constantly to second-guess. Maybe you are good at projecting a decisive attitude by saying what you *don't* want, but you can't articulate what you *do* want. Fear and doubt, the evil twins we'll talk more about later in the book, are the enemies of choice. Do whatever you must to get rid of them. Call the shrink, exorcist, or exterminator and eliminate them from your existence.

Traits of Today's Free Agents

1. Self-aware, introspective, and ego in check
2. Image consistent with who they seek to be
3. Able to articulate experiences, skills, and competencies
4. Build relationships, network effectively, and reciprocate
5. Test reputation, seek and integrate feedback
6. Focused and committed to a few specific roles or industries
7. Proactive and discerning about identifying possible new opportunities

I'm flipping the script: It is up to you to choose your job and find an employer worthy of what you are offering. It is important, though, not to confuse worthiness with entitlement. No one owes you anything, but you certainly are worthy of choosing where you work and how you deploy your skills. This isn't about arrogance. It relates to the convergence I described earlier in which you, as an employee or small business owner, are claiming what you want in order to be productive. Double bonus: Employers and vendors get to have the most productive, cost-effective, and fulfilled employees on their teams.

People who don't make decisions for themselves wind up in the workplace equivalent of a bus tour across Europe with 50 strangers. It's easy, spoon-fed, and you don't have to think for yourself, but you miss the hundreds of special, unique moments you might have experienced if you'd been willing to think through the trip and make your own decisions.

Free agents exercise choice. Adopt the free-agency mindset and you'll bring your "A game" to work and be set up to win in the new economy.

levels

Entry Level

Your expectations about the work world will likely have to change. Even though you might not think you have much leverage or ability to choose, in fact you have quite a bit. Use your youthful innocence to your advantage and just go for what you want with purpose.

Mid-Level

Establish your regimen of building your arsenal of skills, contacts, and other resources. Challenge yourself to learn something new every day, no matter how seemingly insignificant. How do you eat an elephant...?

Executive Level

By now you have probably worked in a few different companies and environments, and you know what you want and what works best for you. Make informed choices and continually evaluate options—even if you don't choose to pursue them.

Encore Level

It is hoped that you have made wise career choices, but perhaps you haven't explored more of what turns out to be an infinite set of possibilities. Push the limits on the "what if" to see where it can lead you.

Detour Route

Introspection is your friend as you right your course. Get in touch with what moves you—with what has meaning—and let that inform your choices. Couple that insight with decision, and you are off to the races.

2

→ SETTING THE TARGET

"Men nearly always follow the tracks made by others and proceed in their affairs by imitation, even though they cannot entirely keep to the tracks of others or emulate the prowess of their models. So a prudent man should always follow in the footsteps of great men and imitate those who have been outstanding. If his own prowess fails to compare with theirs, at least it has an air of greatness about it. He should behave like those archers who, if they are skillful, when the target seems too distant, know the capabilities of their bow and aim a good deal higher than their objective, not in order to shoot so high but so that by aiming high they can reach the target."
~ Niccolò Machiavelli

| The Aerial View

More is not better when a few is enough. I'm a believer in infinite possibilities and in creating choices. However, when it comes to job-hunting and career decisions, I think people have a tendency to think more choices are better, but this is often not the case. I've watched people spend countless hours applying for opportunities on job boards and chasing hiring managers and recruiters when they have failed to ask three fundamental questions:

1. What do I really want—at least at this stage of my life?
2. Am I well suited to perform that role?
3. Am I willing to do what it will take to get me into that role?

Filling your days responding to openings might feel productive, but if you haven't answered the three questions above honestly before you invest energy in applying, you are wasting precious time that could be spent creating and executing a more productive strategy. Having three or four real opportunities that are truly promising and desirable is better than having 15 or 20 possibilities that have a low probability of coming to fruition. It's the proverbial rifle versus shotgun approach: The shotgun's pellets spread out and cover a wide area, but they don't travel very far or very accurately; the bullet from a rifle flies far and true, making it better suited to bigger, faster targets.

> ### Tip
>
> The same logic applies when seeking to develop new clients. Go after the ones you really want, because you can do good work for them. They will be far more likely to be good clients and will enhance your billings and your brand.

You have to build activity and cast a wide net, but you also have to make sure you are fishing in the right waters. Trust me, you are a more attractive candidate (or vendor or service provider) when you are focused, intentional about what you want, and can express your unique set of skills, competencies, and services concisely and clearly.

- Be proactive in deciding what you want, not just reacting to "what's out there."
- Don't put all your eggs in one basket; you must pursue multiple opportunities at once.
- Don't compare yourself to others—ever!
- Know your strengths, where you are, and where you are planning to go.

Let's look at this another way. When you look at a funnel from above, it looks essentially like a target. Envision the outer rings of this target. In darts and archery, hits in these areas earn fewer points than the bull's-eye, but at least you are in the game.

Similarly, we are starting with the outer rings on the target known as your career. Most people jump right into aiming for the bull's-eye by trying to find a role. Usually they get a lot of hits on the wall and miss the target completely. You might say all that matters is that you eventually hit the target. I won't argue that point, but I prefer to increase my chances of hitting it by being in the right room, having my own customized target, and moving closer to the bull's-eye with every shot.

Stay with me here and I promise to get you in the game quickly, but it is crucial that you work through every step to get the most benefit from the process. Why, you ask? Not for my benefit; it is for you. You need to set parameters for yourself or you will bounce around like a foosball or keep missing the target entirely. Just as the magic in the throw of a dart is in the flick of the wrist, the magic in determining your target is that you are consciously choosing the focus of your interest based on things that matter to you and only you.

| Plot Your History

Before you can decide where you are going, you need to look at your past to know whence you've come and what lessons you have learned. Don't make this hard; go with the facts. Pull out your résumé and start to fill in the map (see the map template on page 157). Work first on the industry "verticals," as I like to call them, then work on filling in functions, former roles, and competencies.

We have not yet covered the definitions for all of those, so if you need help, you will find a more detailed explanation and examples of functions, roles, and competencies later in this chapter.

| Industries

In working with a 25-year-old client who lost his job during a massive layoff at IBM, we started by plotting his past jobs. We called IBM—Vertical #1A—"Office Products." Then we included "College/Academics" and "Extracurriculars" as substitutes for other past industries; those two became Vertical #2A and Vertical #3A, respectively. We used his undergraduate degree in finance and his participation in music and sports to direct us to new industries and functions.

He likes to build computers, so technology was a field of interest to him that related to his first job, and Vertical #1B became "Technology." His father had worked in financial services (which typically includes real estate, investment banking, asset management, insurance, and commercial banking), and that area interested him. That gave us Vertical #2B, "Financial Services."

When I asked about his primary passions, he brightened and referred to his college activities—music and sports. He went on to say he would love to work in either of those industries, but he had never thought about it before.

"Great! A dream job starts with a dream," I told him. He filled in Vertical #3B with "Sports and Entertainment."

Lastly, he thought consulting could be interesting, but he wasn't sure of the exact role he might play there. "No problem," I said. "This is just a starting point, and we can change, add, and delete as we go along." Now we had Vertical #4B: "Professional Services."

How do you know which industries make sense for you? Start with where you are now (or where you were most recently) and plot that industry. Look at the other industries you have worked in. Leave out the ones that no longer interest you or that you don't think are growing.

Check the companies' websites, Hoover's, Yahoo Finance, and other resources to find out which primary industry companies consider themselves to be in. Which industries or sectors are related to the ones you have worked in? For example, if you have been in retail (Bloomingdales, Macys, The Gap), you might consider consumer packaged goods (Kraft, Procter & Gamble, Pepsi). If you have worked in government, consider academia or the not-for-profit world. Much will depend on the organization, the function, and the role you will play, but for now, make your top industry picks—no more than four—and we'll move on.

| Companies

At this point you might be thinking that your guide has lost her way. Am I really telling you to select the companies you want to work for after one of the worst recessions in recent generations, one that brought with it record job losses? Yes, I am!

My clients and I used this approach when I worked as a recruiter, crafting our search strategy by first determining the related industries and/or functions most relevant to the search. Then we would drill down and select companies in those industries that were the most attractive based on reputation, geography, and other factors. We would go on to see if there were people we already knew at those companies in the relevant function and level, then we'd supplement the list by researching the names of other people in certain roles at those companies.

Do you see the parallel? You are determining your industries and companies (and, later, your functions and roles) so that you can approach the selected companies to inquire about opportunities—opportunities that aren't necessarily posted.

The other reason for you to select your "favorite" companies is that you will force yourself to learn as much as possible about those companies and make a more informed decision about wanting to work there. You also increase the likelihood of finding an opportunity that actually suits you, rather than the position they might offer if you write in blindly. And when you do land that interview, you will dazzle the interviewer with your in-depth knowledge of the company and industry, and you'll be able to give a compelling rationale for why you are so well-suited for the company's culture, strategy, etc.

Research companies in your targeted industries, and select them based on some of the following criteria:

- Reputation as employers
- Profitability
- Growth potential
- Geography
- Relative compensation

- Environmental commitment
- Firsthand interface with the company as a competitor, vendor, etc.

Whittle the list down to those companies you can really see yourself working for, and don't overlook your current employer. There could be one or two unexplored possibilities right under your nose.

| Functions

Functions in the workplace are categories that describe your broad skills base or expertise. Forget about level and rank for a moment. Functional categories tend to mirror the boxes on a company's organizational chart and can include finance, marketing, sales, human resources, operations, business development, strategy, information technology, research, supply chain/logistics, and general management, to name a few. The general management function is typically reserved for a supervisor or other leader responsible for a profit and loss statement and/or for people who oversee a variety of functions (e.g., division manager, president, etc.).

My coaching client had been working in marketing but was more interested in finance (in which he has his degree), specifically strategy or risk management. He considered the field of information technology (IT) based on his prowess with computers, but after reviewing some IT job specifications, he didn't see himself doing that work all day every day.

Some functions can take you to other places you might want to be. It is often the case that operations, finance, strategy, and marketing functions can take people to the "C-suite" in a company. ("C-suite" refers to the officer level of a company, the level at which people have the word *chief* in their titles.) If getting to the top is your long-term goal, know that there is no singular path.

For now, choose the functions that appeal to you most, as those are the ones that are more likely to help you develop greater expertise, seniority, and satisfaction. Don't allow yourself to be locked into doing only what you have done in the past! Fill in the map in two places: one near the top of the first page for past jobs, and the other under your new verticals.

| Roles and Titles

This is the fun part for me. I think many of us are problem solvers by nature, and this is free-form problem solving at its best. Get online and look for job postings and descriptions that interest you in your chosen function. Start with some of your target companies.

But: *You are not applying for these jobs—yet!* You are assembling prototype job specifications for the industries and functions you have chosen using the information from some of your favorite companies. So have fun with this. To complete this part of your career map, you can search websites of targeted companies and career sites like Monster, CareerBuilder, etc.

In addition to online research, attend conferences and job fairs, and review your current or most recent position description if it is something you love doing. The map is flexible, and you can fill it with as much of the following as you like for each of the industry verticals you have selected and for each of the functional segments in those industries:

- Titles of past jobs
- Historical roles played in not-for-profits, professional associations, churches, and other outside organizations
- "Aspirational" roles you see yourself playing in the future

Once again, it is vitally important to be thorough with this one. When I was an executive recruiter, one of the most frustrating things people would do to me was to thrust their résumés in my face and ask, "What do you think?"

I would sometimes respond with the question, "What do you want me to think?"

The point is, no one can tell you what you should be doing. You must tell a potential employer, and you must have a rationale for what you tell them. If you are lacking in experience and/or trying to make a transition to another industry or function, learning how to articulate what you are aiming for becomes even more critical.

Now you are equipped with the language that your favorite companies use to describe roles you want to perform. You have an understanding of the levels or ranking in the organizational structure, and you can tell someone you see yourself "entering at the managerial level in the IT applications group, which appears to interface heavily with the operations function." This is far more compelling than a candidate who expresses interest in IT but demonstrates no knowledge of levels, responsibilities, or other aspects of the job.

You are making great headway, and even if you are not actively looking for a new job, career mapping is still an amazing exercise to help you assess for yourself how you are coming in your career—regardless of whether or not you have an expressed goal. You might even conclude that the goal you thought you had is no longer realistic based on how your interests and skills have changed and developed.

The next phase of the career mapping process will take you through some qualitative analysis that might seem a little "touchy-feely" but is vitally important because it will help you identify and address some behaviors that inhibit or even sabotage your ability to create opportunities for yourself. At this point you have prepared the outline of your stories, and now you are going to compile the guts of the stories with this qualitative assessment.

By the way, if you don't like the map template, you can use a notebook or notepad to capture all of this information thoroughly. It is too complex to commit to memory, and there are many key words and concepts you'll want to refer back to as the process is completed.

Entry Level

This might feel very fanciful and dreamy since you don't have a lot of experience to base your choices on. The key is to listen to your inner voice and learn what really appeals to you, not anyone else. Balance that with detailed research on the companies and roles so you are making fact-based decisions.

Mid-Level

You could be inclined to stay really focused at this level because you might have moved around earlier or because you think the only way to move up is to keep doing what you have been doing. Don't box yourself in. Live a little, and explore industries and functions that are closely related to the ones you have been in—even if you learn only enough to know you don't want them.

Executive Level

If you are like me, you have a substantial number of years under your belt and might feel a bit overwhelmed, self-conscious, or annoyed plotting all of this information on the map. Trust me, the process is worth the effort. You will see patterns and a forward path more clearly. In forming my own business after leaving executive search, I used these plotting methods, and over time I've been able to articulate the lines of business that make sense for me.

Encore Level

Like the entry-level person above, you might feel that this is fanciful and dreamy; not because you lack experience, but because you have so much experience and have less at stake. You might be in a position to "stop and smell the flowers" for the first time in a long time, and this process will allow you to do that without going too far afield. Follow the advice I gave the entry-level applicant: Listen to your inner voice, and find you what you really want, then research specific organizations and roles that might be a good fit. In other words, be sure to balance whimsy with fact.

Detour Route

If there is one group for which this process is most important, it is you! You are trying to get back on track. Whether it's a new track or an old one, you need to tell true stories that illustrate self-awareness, clarity, and decisiveness. You simply don't have the luxury of leaving things to chance.

3

EXPLORING YOUR PERSONAL GEOGRAPHY

"Your time is limited, so don't waste it living someone else's life. Don't be trapped by dogma—which is living with the results of other people's thinking. Don't let the noise of others' opinions drown out your own inner voice. And most important, have the courage to follow your heart and intuition. They somehow already know what you truly want to become. Everything else is secondary." ~ Steve Jobs

Now that you have marked your target and made some of the tough and not-so-tough choices about industry, companies, functions, and roles, it is time to develop more precision. A common mistake people make when describing themselves in a professional context is to launch into a list of their current and past jobs and experience. This list, however, is the hastily sketched map a clerk at a convenience store might draw on a napkin when you stop to ask for directions. I'm asking you to create a full-color map that reflects the geography of the real you—the *who you are*—with all the color and richness that only you can provide.

| Inventories

Countless aptitude, personality, and psychometric tests and inventories that have considerable merit can serve as helpful signposts at this juncture in your journey. Here are a few of the most well-known: Myers-Briggs Type Indicator, Johnson O'Conner Research Foundation aptitude testing, and StrengthsFinder 2.0.

I typically use StrengthsFinder 2.0 with my coaching clients; the descriptors are generally accurate, and while they don't make explicit recommendations as to which jobs you are best suited for, they can force you to give thought to the identified traits or tendencies and accept or reject them. You will walk away with greater clarity and insight into yourself, which is the endgame.

The themes and output from an individual's StrengthsFinder 2.0 test (as an example) can provide language that helps match that person with job descriptions. Try taking a few different tests, assessments, and inventories; compare and contrast the results, and you might even ask a friend or colleague which descriptors best fit you. Lay out your results beside your career map, and let's continue filling in the next several lines on the map to add some color and shading to your personal geography.

Here are some themes that came from my StrengthsFinder 2.0 inventory. I found them to be spot-on and helpful in amplifying the language I now use to describe myself:

1. Strategic problem solver, analytical, can spot patterns and issues, able to generate options and innovative ideas.
2. Connector or bridge with curiosity about diverse points of view, facilitator.
3. Results-oriented, driven and determined to achieve goals and help others do the same through partnerships and friendships.
4. Communicator and messenger who calls others to action. Plainspoken approach eliminates ambiguity. Someone who takes charge and is a trusted leader, counselor, and advisor.
5. Instinctive and independent, self-reliant but willing to work with and through teams. Also committed to pursuing education and personal growth.

| Competencies

"Competencies" is an often bandied about term that is not always differentiated from other words used to describe what you do and have done. I view competencies as skills, knowledge, and capabilities explained in context. Competencies are not just what you've been responsible for or do well; they provide the context and dimension for what you do and how you do it. For example, you can say you are a "strong leader who has led teams of 20-30 people."

A better description of your leadership competency might be to say:

"I have gotten great results, both in sales and morale, leading my sales teams by setting clear benchmarks, going out in the field with all of my people semi-annually, and maintaining several large accounts myself to stay current on customer trends."

Another person might say:

"In leading my operations team of 20, I find I get the best results from my people by encouraging them to forge strong relationships with their internal customers while I remain a technical resource for them as they need me. I also run interference for them and keep them informed of leadership and strategic decisions that affect them."

Do you see the "how" in the latter descriptions? If you were the hiring manager, which candidate would appeal to you more? One of the key words in both of the lengthier descriptions is "results," which justifies saying you are a "strong leader." "Results" answers the question, "What makes you strong?"

Let me tell you a story about another one of my coaching clients. Her experience is broad and spotty. Her life has taken many turns, and what started as a career turned into a foray into entrepreneurship, then a series of jobs to support her children after her divorce and in the wake of her mother's death. She did her undergraduate work in art history at an elite women's college and expected to pursue her love of design, art, and creative expression in some form. She started as a fashion buyer after college and went on to work for several retailers in that capacity in the next seven years. This suited her; she loved the work, she developed good managerial skills, and she used her great design eye to display items on the store floors attractively. But this was 20 years ago.

In the intervening years she joined her mother in a gourmet food business (which failed), trained as a pastry chef, and co-founded a food product marketing and demonstration company (providing food sampling at retailers like Whole Foods). She also got both of her children through private school and into college. Most recently she secured a job with a real estate developer in an administrative assistant/marketing assistant role. Rather predictably, the real estate development business weakened with the economy, and Lucy's position was eliminated. She never got to learn the leasing business as she'd hoped, but she gained a few other administrative and communication skills.

What we have here is a bit of a patchwork quilt of experiences for this woman in her early 50s. She has done considerable introspection with therapists and spiritualists to cope with the questions, losses, and occasional confusion in her life. Now she is more resolute, confident, and optimistic than she has ever been. Nevertheless, she has struggled with setting priorities and identifying roles, competencies, and gaps that will allow her to settle on one function or role for the balance of her work life. In a word, she is overwhelmed.

Lucy's StrengthsFinder 2.0 inventory revealed some of the following themes:

1. **Watches people to know what special gifts and traits they can bring to a situation.** Figures out how to work with people who are different.   Partners well on a team.
2. **Turns thoughts into action; frustrated by delays.** Willing to act when others won't, but can convince others to participate based on the value she sees them bringing to the situation.
3. **Seeks to improve continuously through learning.** Anxious to expand thinking, comprehend new ideas, and gain skills.
4. **Contemplates the future.** Inspired by possibilities of success and ability to use natural gifts.
5. **Takes ownership and is committed to delivering on all commitments.** Mature and able to admit shortcomings as well as acknowledge her expertise.

For the purposes of your career map, you will use only a few words to describe your competencies, but we will work on the longer version for elements of your résumé, your elevator pitch, and your interview responses. Go ahead and list at least two competencies for each historical role and for the "aspirational" roles on your map.

| Gaps

Gap analysis can be a tough thing to do. The inclination might be to have someone else tell you where you fall short, or you might become discouraged when you see you don't have everything a job requires. It is important that you know where you are in terms of competencies and experiences, that you have a plan to fill the gaps when possible, and that you develop the language to address your gaps when talking to prospective employers.

It sounds straightforward, but how do you know exactly what your gaps are? There is no other way than to look in the mirror and be honest with yourself; you must be as objective and unemotional as possible in your self-assessment. Very often what you perceive as a competency gap is in fact an experience gap that you can address with a competency you have deployed in another context.

Lucy chose retail, hospitality, and public relations as three of her verticals, and marketing, merchandizing, sales, and communications as her functional areas. These seemed like good choices based on her past experience, training, and exposure.

In order to determine some of her gaps, Lucy visited the websites of some of her target companies to get job descriptions for positions in her specific functional areas. She did not apply for these jobs, but together we analyzed the job descriptions to determine which roles she could realistically perform. Several conclusions emerged:

- **Lucy is not qualified to go into marketing, except at the lowest level.** She has no training or academic exposure, no advertising experience or contacts, and no quantitative analytical aptitude. Too many gaps, most of which she can't fill; we wiped this function off the list across verticals.
- **Visual merchandizing appears to be a nice fit.** Lucy did this early in her career, but she has maintained her creative and artistic eye, most recently deploying this talent in the culinary arts world. Depending on an employer's expectations for computer prowess, she might fill her gap in that area with a class to be more competitive. Her résumé did not include the words "visual merchandizing," so we made a note to include the phrase in her customized "retail/fashion/merchandizing" résumé.

- **Assistant and associate buyer roles at two companies were appealing based on Lucy's early work as a buyer.** One had a distinctly operational, inventory-oriented bent, however, and the other, more senior role required high-level cross-functional interface, market analysis, and management of field teams. Both roles would be far too senior for her, and in spite of her previous "buyer" titles with attractive companies, this function is not something she wants to try to grow into over the next few years.
- **Communications is a function much like marketing that one typically learns through a degree program and job experience.** Lucy has never developed public relations materials or communications plans or programs. She is a good writer and oral communicator but has not presented in front of large groups. A writing or presentation skills course probably won't get her up to speed quickly enough.
- **Lucy identified a public relations firm in the Bay Area (where she lived at the time) that interested her.** There didn't seem to be any open positions, but we scanned the service offerings of the company to see how they were structured. There were three groups: core business services (media planning, etc.), writing services (e.g., press releases) and event services (event planning and society receptions and dinners). Event planning services jumped off the page for both of us. It encompassed her culinary expertise, her creative bent, and her organizational and detail competencies. She can easily make a case for herself in this role. This was not one of the functions or roles she initially considered, but it is one that she is prepared to pursue.
- **Hospitality appealed to Lucy because of the strong food and design elements.** She looked at marketing roles in this vertical, but she just didn't have the qualifications. However, most hotels do have event planning functions, and Lucy decided hotels would be the first places she would look for such roles. She also decided she only wanted to approach high-end hotels to align with her sophisticated and creative taste in food and design.

After we finished this exercise, Lucy was quiet for a moment. Then she started nodding to herself and said, "I like this. I can do this." We ended our session with a homework assignment in which Lucy would work on her elevator pitch. She called back 15 minutes later to say she was thrilled to have carved out a new role for herself that she had never before considered. She did it herself by plotting her history and making choices for her industries, functions, and roles. She went ahead and filled out the career map with her target companies and contacts because she was so excited with her new ability to see how she was going to create opportunities for herself.

| Fear and Doubt

Some people won't budge unless the weather is perfect. Fear and doubts are like the storms and fog that keep us from moving ahead.

Fear, some say, can be a motivator. I don't agree. On a good day fear imposes limits on your thoughts, imagination, and aspirations; on a bad day, it can be utterly debilitating. I urge you to confront those fears that have been getting in the way of your success as you define it.

Common job and career fears are rejection, acceptance (counter-intuitive but common), poverty, and failure. Your fears can take the form of dubious questions you ask or statements you make to yourself. For instance:

- What will the family say?
- I'm not like people currently in the role.
- Am I really ready to do what it takes?
- I feel like an impostor.
- It's risky, and I'm risk averse.

These questions and statements masquerade as rational, cautious sentiments, but they can paralyze you to the point of inaction. If you are really stuck and can't seem to figure out why you are so fearful, seek help. I offer this advice often, and I mean it from the heart. Developing the ability to create a career strategy and implement successful tactics to realize your career goals will far outweigh any short-term discomfort, expense, and/ or embarrassment that results from seeking therapy or counseling. Once the fog has lifted, you'll be able to see the path ahead much more clearly.

A word on doubt. It is fear's best friend and is a bit like mold in terms of its ability to permeate and overtake a space. You can defy innate pessimistic tendencies by learning to trust in yourself, your skills, and your beliefs. You can learn to live with the uncertainty of not knowing how something will turn out by pushing through the doubt to maintain confidence and faith that it will turn out for the best. Do not let doubt or fear lead to inaction. Drive through the dark moments into the light of your conviction. Presume that there are people and forces out there conspiring for your success—but only if you push the ball forward.

Lucy was afraid to get her master of fine arts (MFA) degree after she graduated from college 30 years ago. She had watched her mother struggle as a fashion designer in spite of being enormously talented; her mother's ideas just didn't seem to work. Lucy's conclusion was that "creatives" struggle in the real world. Despite her fear of pursuing the degree, she stayed true to her passions and gifts by continuing to seek out jobs that had creative elements—mostly in food preparation and retail sales.

Now Lucy is facing two other overarching fears, one having to do with her age, and the other having to do with her relative lack of recent experience in any one area. These are valid concerns because we live in a youth-conscious society—even though demographics in many countries suggest that a shortage of younger workers will force companies to hire older, "encore" workers. As for the experience piece, we are in a competitive job market where people with considerable experience are finding it difficult to get work. The fact is that Lucy can't change either of these conditions.

She is 52, and her work experience is what it is. Her choice is to stare down the existing conditions and blow past them with a clear strategy and her career map in hand. Thanks to her map, Lucy can express clearly her skills and competencies and confidence in her wisdom and ability to outperform others who might have more experience. Or she can be tentative about what she can contribute, apologize for her age and work history, and diminish her chances of getting hired because of her lack of confidence. Which would you choose?

| Courage and Choice

The opposite of fear is courage. (Others say love, but that's another discussion). Throughout your life you have to draw upon courage to move out of your comfort zone and achieve what you want. Whether it is standing up to the bully who took your lunch money, asking the attractive person out on a date, or deciding to leave your job and/or change careers, courage can take many forms. We all have courage in varying degrees, in different areas of our lives, and at different points in our lives. Youth can impart a false sense of courage that can take the form of irresponsibility or impetuousness. Maturity can mean we might feel locked in, having few choices because of perceived irrevocable obligations.

My view is that we always have choices—always. The choices might not be desirable at the time, but they remain viable choices. What often differentiates the person who is successful from the one who isn't is the courage to pose the almighty question, "What if?"

I asked myself the "What if?" question in early 2009. I had been with Spencer Stuart nearly 12 years and really enjoyed being an executive recruiter, but I started this book in 2003, and I wanted to finish it. I had it in my mind that I would be more desirable to publishers if I stayed with the firm. The problem was that there were no precedents for the type of book I was writing. Other partners in the firm had written books on leadership but not career management. Also, the economy dictated that every revenue-generating consultant needed to be pounding the pavement to drum up business.

This meant I wouldn't have much time to finish writing the book, much less to go on book tours and do media events. After an introspective weekend alone, I asked myself, *What if? What if I were to leave the firm, complete my book on my own, and start a consulting and coaching business?*

I had never asked myself this question before, and it was scary. Once I asked it of myself, a stream of scenarios came to mind in response to the question. If I left, I would have extra time to spend with my teenage son; they say children need you more in their teens than when they are younger. As a traveling single mother, I regularly fended off guilt about being away from Julian, and there was no substitute for being present in his life more days out of the week than not.

Leaving Spencer Stuart would enable me to explore a move into media. The firm frowned upon individual promotion and favored maintaining a cohesive corporate brand. By forming a consulting business, I could stay close to my passion for talent management and corporate diversity, but not necessarily do executive search. I had begun to feel that the transactional nature of search didn't allow for real cultural transformation within an organization. All of these things took on new importance as I looked down the yellow brick road. This was not Kansas anymore, and I was not dreaming.

Once I asked the "What if?" question, I started to get "messages" from unexpected places reinforcing the fact that my decision was likely the right one for me. I shared my thinking about possibly leaving with a friend, and she said, "When you are standing on a cliff preparing to jump, you need to remember that if you have faith (or courage), you will either land on something soft or learn to fly." I thought to myself, "I am not landing on anything, no matter how soft; I'm flying!"

The other message was from my cousin, Patricia, who worked in bank operations (teller services) for 40 years. She has known me all my life and has watched my career with interest and admiration.

I told her I was thinking about leaving Spencer Stuart. I fully expected her to question the feasibility of that move because I was a single mother. Without missing a beat she responded, "Ginny, whatever you say you are going to do, you do; you have been that way all your life."

"Wow," I thought, "she is right." With few exceptions, I did everything I said I was going to do based on determination (my brother called me "Head" for "headstrong"), resourcefulness, and clarity of mission. My cousin helped me define certain personal traits or attributes that all but ensured my success in my future endeavors. I tendered my resignation the following week and have not had a moment of regret. Anxiety? Uncertainty? Yes. But regret? No!

| Attributes

Unlike your work history and past experiences, which might have gaps related to where you want to be, you have certain personal attributes and characteristics that are absolute; they are truisms that are simply a part of who you are. Just as my cousin helped bring my determination, resourcefulness, and clarity of mission into focus, you are going to identify a few of your own attributes that can even compensate for a lack of experience or competencies.

The fact is that many of the qualities or attributes you have identified can be linked to competencies that led to past successes. As an example, Lucy's creativity and sophisticated taste, coupled with her analytical capacity and results orientation, led her from fashion to food, where she worked only with gourmet products and in fine dining establishments. Not everyone can operate at that level of the food service industry. She can leverage her attributes and exposure into other areas related to a luxury lifestyle (high-end and boutique hotels, luxury retailers, etc.).

I have chosen not to address weaknesses, frailties, and blind spots, as those are often manifestations of fear. You know what they are; you likely confront them every day, if only in your mind. If you don't come face to face with them, you will continue to struggle. But for now I don't want you to focus on any negatives, so go ahead and write down your personal attributes. Be honest, and have fun doing it.

Entry Level

You won't have many proven competencies because you simply don't have the experience to have amassed them. Therefore you need to be able to talk explicitly about your preferences, strengths, and tendencies in certain work-related settings. This can be in the context of teams, committees, volunteer organizations, or internships. Give brief examples of situations where you solved problems, resolved conflicts, or provided an innovative idea.

Mid-Level

At this level your experiences might be narrow, but continuously analyzing your competencies, gaps, and attributes can allow you to tease out skills and strengths that will move you to the next level. Don't wait for someone to identify those characteristics in you; do your own self-assessment regularly, and be prepared to offer yourself up for that role at the next level.

Executive Level

Don't fall victim to complacency. Keep doing your own competency and gap analysis to remain competitive. Even if you have achieved the highest level you sought, be reflective to make sure you are giving all you can to others and continuing to derive personal and professional satisfaction and stimulation from your work

Encore Level

Like Lucy's, sometimes your gaps are not so apparent. For example, job descriptions don't always state expectations for computer proficiency; it's a given. Make sure all aspects of your competencies and skill sets are up to date. If need be, get supplemental training to stay competitive—whether you're employed or not.

Detour Route

Once again, this process is critically important to you because you are weaving a potentially disjointed job history into a coherent story, making up for lost time, and/or dusting off old skills. The common threads are your unique qualities, skills, and strengths and an awareness of what you are best suited for. It is incumbent upon you to tell others what you want and why.

SHIPSHAPE

"IT IS NOT THE MOUNTAIN WE CONQUER BUT OURSELVES." ~ EDMUND HILLARY

4

SHIP-TO-SHORE COMMUNICATION

"There can be no happiness if the things we believe in are different from the things we do." ~ Freya Stark

The woman sitting across the desk from me was interviewing for a C-suite job in finance in which she would report directly to the president of the company. Her qualifications were impeccable. She had a sense of humor, and her razor-sharp mind was evident throughout the interview. But one problem made me question whether to put her on the short list of candidates: her choice of interview outfit.

When she sat down, her blouse pulled tight across her chest and gapped open, and her skirt looked uncomfortably tight. She was clearly aware of it, because she kept trying to cover the gap with a folder she was holding. I estimated that she had looked fine in that outfit about 30 lbs. ago. Now, this is not about discriminating against someone for being overweight; I just wondered if she'd done a mirror check before going out the door.

I did end up sending her to my corporate client for an interview, but I gave the human resources person a heads-up about the candidate's appearance. The candidate showed up for the interview similarly dressed, and she got the position in spite of her appearance. But my first impression was hard to get past, and it made me question how in touch with herself this woman was.

The expression is well worn for a reason: You never get a second chance to make a first impression. Like it or not, you are always on display—whether on paper, on the Internet, on the phone, at social or networking events, in an elevator or lobby, or in a room with an interviewer. How you look, what you say, and how you interact with others speaks volumes about how you see yourself and what kind of employee or business partner you might be.

Once you have done the work of identifying where you are, taking inventory of your target jobs, matching those with an inventory of your competencies, and figuring out where you want to go, you still need to get to your destination.

You are the captain in charge, and your vessel shows off your personal brand. Make sure everything is in good working order. What does the way you present yourself say about you? What finishing touches do you need to be in shipshape?

| Personal Branding

Having a "brand" in the business world is critical—whether you like to think of yourself as a brand or not. I take issue with the notion that it is all about packaging. I'd like to think that business professionals cannot be duped by empty suits and smooth talk.

Your brand can include your tagline, your personal story, and your elevator pitch, but it must have substance. Some people get hired on the basis of their perceived personal brand, but they won't last unless they can deliver on the promise. I think of personal branding as having four components:

- Authenticity
- Reputation
- Image
- Value

The graphic below captures the essence of the personal brand:

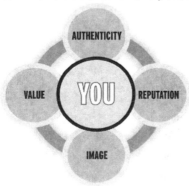

| Authenticity

We spent the first three chapters digging out and dusting off your competencies, so let's add them to a few other elements, experiences, achievements, and aspirations to form the foundation for what you want to be known for—the authentic you:

EXPERIENCES This is where many people start and stop. Recounting the jobs you have had is only the beginning. To me, it feels like snapshots that tell only part of your story. Learn how to weave a (true) story that links one job to another with insight into why and how you made your decisions and choices.

COMPETENCIES With a description of your skills, knowledge, and capabilities, we are starting to tell a story, but it's like looking at a black and white map. You have to be able to distill what you are really good at and how you go about doing things. Offer context; that is, express preferences for and exposure to certain kinds of situations and circumstances that provide dimension and interest to your map.

ACHIEVEMENTS Now the map is colorized with your topography—the successes and "lessons" you have had. Be able to state your role in a winning situation, and talk about what you learned when something went wrong. As an example, were you in a lead or supporting role?

ASPIRATIONS Everyone wants to dream, and dream big you should. Visualize the happy ending. Don't be afraid to express your goals, desires, and ambitions. Not only do I believe you manifest them by claiming them, but others generally want to help you achieve your goals as well. Put them out there!

| Reputation

So now you really can articulate the authentic you. But do you know your reputation, which is what other people say about you? Having achieved and maintained a good reputation adds to your personal brand. If you have a glowing reputation, people will often tell you as much. On the other hand, people generally won't be so helpful as to tell you when you have a "bad rep."

There are three must-haves when building a reputation:

CREDIBILITY People need to know you are trustworthy, have good judgment, and are responsible. Little things like not being punctual or not responding to voicemail and email in a timely fashion can undermine your credibility. Each of these suggests you don't manage time well, are disorganized, or are dismissive. My old firm had an unwritten rule that you always get back to a colleague within 24 hours if possible. You must be attuned to honoring both the spoken and unspoken rules.

CAPABILITY This is the horsepower to get the job done; it's "what's between your ears." Subject matter expertise is always valued, but so is problem solving. You do not necessarily have to have already demonstrated or experienced something, but it is the process of figuring out how to accomplish a task that is important.

COMMITMENT Having the first two attributes without your heart and head in the game won't cut it. This part of the formula can take the form of work ethic, passion, or plain tenacity. Commitment can be demonstrated in many ways, but it is almost always perceptible to all.

How do you know your reputation? What is said behind your back? and who can be honest. In addition, quiz colleagues for "in the moment" assessments after a meeting or presentation. When *you* are asked, provide constructive, thoughtful, and objective feedback to others; this paves the way for them to do the same for you.

- Leverage formal performance review processes to dig deeper and find out more than what might be offered. In addition to your direct supervisor, seek input from sponsors, mentors, and advisors both internal and external to your company or group.
- Consider the source. There are "haters" out there who will be ultra-critical because they don't like you or secretly want to see you fail. There are also those who just won't get you. Go with the law of averages and take the prevailing commentary to heart—good or bad.

Early in my career, a boss who had developed a reputation around the office for his temper berated me because he felt I contradicted him in a client meeting. After the meeting I followed him into his office and closed the door behind me. "First of all, I feel strongly that I did not contradict you," I said firmly. "Secondly, I'm a grown woman, and please don't ever speak to me again in that manner. You can be either part of the solution or part of the problem when it comes to my progress up the learning curve. Right now you are part of the problem."

To his credit, he sought feedback from a number of other colleagues and heard the same message from them. He consciously worked on changing what could have been a serious impediment to his career ascension. He made radical changes in his management style, working to become much more tolerant of differing opinions and to gain control of his infamous temper. He has since become a successful leader and commands great respect and admiration from his peers as well as his direct reports.

Comport yourself in a manner consistent with the reputation you want to have; it is not easy to change your reputation once word is out. Brass can be polished with some elbow grease, but once something is dented or scratched, it must be replaced or overhauled completely, which takes time. If you do need to change your reputation, here are some tips:

VISIBILITY Sometimes not having left any impression is a bad impression. Even if you are an introvert, find ways to make yourself known. Don't force it, or you won't be convincing, but do give some thought to ways you can call positive attention to yourself. If, for example, you are great with numbers but don't like the limelight, offer to be the analyst for a project or the finance person for a committee or project. Attend conferences, and if you are senior and credible enough, offer to moderate or serve on a panel to let people see how knowledgeable you are on your subject matter.

MESSAGING Words are powerful, but actions can often speak louder than words. Make sure you are conveying the right messages about the three C's—credibility, capability, and commitment. Be consistent with everyone you meet. Walk the talk, and demonstrate that you are who you say you are. Avoid hyperbole, but be careful not to present false modesty either.

THOUGHT LEADERSHIP Capturing your ideas in a paper, article, blog, or presentation can go a long way toward establishing or re-establishing your reputation. Make sure the ideas are your ideas—or at least attribute them properly. You don't want to develop a reputation for being a poacher or, worse yet, a plagiarist.

HUMILITY Some people have developed a reputation for being arrogant, users, steamrollers, generally difficult to work with, or just plain mean. Even those people can "find religion" and change their ways. Make amends with people, and ask for forgiveness. Learn the power of establishing personal connections; offer to assist, and show your vulnerability and compassion *before* you need to ask for help.

When I was recruiting, I was often approached by top-level executives eager for the prestige and monetary compensation that comes with a seat on a corporate board. One man, a management consultant in his 60s, was baffled as to why he wasn't flooded with invitations to serve on boards. After all, he ran a successful firm and served on several nonprofit boards. He thought he was overdue.

"I just don't understand," he told me over lunch. "I see all these idiots getting on boards, and we both know I'm better than they are."

"Harold, do you know what your reputation is like?" I asked as diplomatically as I could.

"What are you talking about, Ginny? My reputation is sterling," he barked.

What my lunch companion did not know was that he had developed a dubious reputation in business for his gift of making a lot of money—all at the expense of others. He was reviled for being self-serving and taking credit for the ideas of his junior executives—many of whom had gone on to be wildly successful at other companies. Harold had many high-level acquaintances, but no one ever told him (or he had not heard them when they told him) that his reputation was a liability. It was a case of the emperor wearing no clothes.

"It's good you've done all these wonderful things on these non-profit boards, but what do people say about you?" I pressed, aware that I was putting our friendship at risk. And, true to his reputation, he got angry with me.

"When you've been around as long as I have, you're bound to make some enemies," he snapped and called for the check.

I could only hope that he would reflect on my feedback, but I don't think he ever took a hard look in the mirror. When you always put yourself first, it catches up with you eventually.

Money alone won't get you into the right circles. Lucy, my coaching client from Chapter 3, wanted to raise her visibility in the elite social circles in her community. She does not have seniority, money, or status, but she does have pedigree, polish, and contacts.

These characteristics play well in her chosen role of event planner, and she has decided to pursue opportunities with only the most exclusive hotels and event planning companies in the area. Her confidence has soared now that she, at age 52, has a plan to build her professional reputation based on things she does well and that mean something to her.

| Image

Managing your image is a critical part of establishing and maintaining your personal brand. There is surely no substitute for content or the ingredients of your brand; but, as we discussed at the beginning of this chapter, if the packaging isn't right, you won't get a second look.

Here are the elements that constitute your image. You never know when someone is watching, so whether at the grocery store or a conference, make your mother proud.

APPEARANCE Impressions are formed in seconds, not minutes. Your clothing, hair, and grooming tell someone much about how you see yourself. Understand the environment you are operating in, and stay within the boundaries of appropriateness. Know what "business casual" means in Des Moines versus Florida and at a software firm versus an investment bank. It doesn't take a lot of money to present yourself professionally. Clothing and shoes must fit and should be in good repair; shoes must be clean and shined. Hair must be clean and styled, nails trimmed and clean.

SPEECH Whether in casual conversation or making a presentation, the way you speak can determine the level of attention you can command. Be articulate, passionate, and confident. You don't need to be loud to be heard. You do need to use excellent grammar, straightforward vocabulary, and speak clearly, succinctly, and deliberately. Leave out the extraneous (non)words such as "um," "like," "sort of," "you know," etc. Consider recording yourself and then listening for poor habits in your patterns of speech.

BEHAVIOR Think about people you are attracted to in large settings. What is it that draws you to them? Usually it is eye contact, a smile, and positive energy that makes them approachable. They show a genuine interest in others. Wallflowers convey shyness and a lack of confidence. Bulldozers are boorish, pushy, and sometimes mask a lack of confidence. How do you think you are perceived in a social setting or in the workplace?

AUTHENTICITY You can't be who you aren't. It's about being comfortable in your own skin. As Jay-Z says, "Do you, already." Nothing turns me off more than seeing someone who is disingenuous, insincere, or just plain phony.

| Value

"A brand's value is a financial representation of a business's earnings due to the superior demand created for its products and services through the strength of its brand."
~ Interbrand Corporation

When it comes to your personal brand, your value is harder to measure and is far more subjective. Your job is to help others see the value that you bring by having a realistic sense of what that value is.

Your understanding of the value you bring should be based on objective input, context, demand, and remuneration. Here's what I mean:

CONTEXT You need to learn the conditions in which your attributes are best deployed. I have worked in more than one place where the organization and I simply ceased to be compatible, usually because my skills were not completely valued. In one case it was a matter of company culture: I knew I would not be allowed to move up to the level I wanted to attain. In another situation, I found that I no longer agreed with the company strategy. When your work environment becomes discordant and you are no longer seen or valued, re-plant yourself in another group or another company—or start your own.

DEMAND AND REMUNERATION Are they related? It's great to be wanted, and it's important to know your worth. The reality is that in most organizations, until you reach the loftiest heights, you are bound by compensation restrictions regardless of how wonderful you are. Pay your dues and keep performing; you are investing in yourself. In the meantime, learn how to secure non-financial remuneration for a job well done. This can take the form of a promotion, title upgrade (not always a promotion), access to educational opportunities, increased responsibilities, and much more.

VALUE PROPOSITION Tell, don't ask. Only you know what you are capable of and what you are willing to add to the party. Be prepared to tell people what that is—without apologies. This isn't about being boastful or arrogant, but it is about standing up for yourself and making sure you are being appreciated for your contributions. You can't assume that everyone sees your value, at least not in the same way you see it. Many people make the mistake of thinking that simply doing a good job should be enough. It is not. State your worth; if you don't, you'll find that sometimes no one will take notice.

| Affirmations

To affirm something means to validate, to confirm, to state positively; to assert (as a judgment or decree) as valid or confirmed; to express dedication to.

You must affirm who you are to be successful in your life and career. It is more than just lip service. Affirmations are a commitment to internalizing your vision so that it will manifest itself in your life. That sounds a little mystical, I know, but let me give you a practical example of how to use affirmations in your life and career.

I was doing a mock interview with an executive recently, and I expressed to her the importance of leaving 3–5 key points about herself with every interviewer (including the CEO) she would be meeting at the company where she was interviewing that week. I asked her to tell me what three of those important points were. She struggled, and sentences became paragraphs—not key points.

I said, "Stop. Back up and tell me who you are. What makes you uniquely you and qualified for this job? What can you assert or affirm about yourself relative to this opportunity?"

After thinking about it for a few minutes, she was able to express what made her an expert capable of filling this role. I heard from her later that week, and she got the offer. I can't attribute the offer solely to the affirmations, but here's what I know:

- Affirmations solidify in your mind how you see yourself in the world. You are therefore more convincing and compelling to others when expressing your special skills and attributes. If you don't believe it, don't expect me to!
- Affirmations flow into goal-setting; once you can state what you are bringing to a situation, you know where potential gaps are that you need to fill to achieve your goals.
- Affirmations are personal; no one can write them for you. Others can give you input, but you have to know their observations to be true.

Make your affirmations specific and "aspirational." Take time to reflect deeply; more than a brand, this is who you are. I updated my list of affirmations recently. Here's one of them:
"I am an expert and thought-leader on the subjects of organizational talent management and personal career management."

Not everyone in the world knows and acknowledges this yet, but I do, and that is where it starts.

| Perfecting the Elevator Pitch

One of the most important parts of your job search is being able to tell someone about yourself in only a couple of minutes—the length of an elevator ride. It's like a miniature spoken résumé, a verbal business card. It is not only an opportunity to extend your personal brand, it is a chance to hear yourself affirm your own merits. We went to great pains in Section I of this book to tease out key words and phrases that define you in different contexts:

- **In the specific industries and functions you chose, you found language that is common and unique to those industries and functions.** For example, the marketing function in a consumer goods company involves activities such as branding, channels, and promotions, while marketing in the hospitality industry involves direct/Internet marketing, collateral materials, and more.
- **In choosing roles that comprise your two or three prototypes, you found key words and phrases that recurred in several job descriptions; start to own these.**
- **Writing your affirmations provided even more adjectives and nouns that lend further clarity to how you want to be known and perceived.**

What exactly would you say if you found yourself on an elevator or at a cocktail party with the hiring manager for a job you really want—and you only had two minutes? Here are some do's and don'ts to help perfect your pitch:

- Don't try to cram your entire career into 60 seconds.
- Do give highlights of your most prestigious and recent roles, including company name and title.
- Don't assume people know or understand your expertise.
- Do describe and quantify—industry segment, budget, revenues, number of employees.
- Don't oversell or ask favors—you are meeting for the first time.
- Do be clear about what you think your strengths are.
- Don't be one-dimensional in your commentary.
- Do offer an interesting personal fact about yourself.

I recently met a woman at an event where I was speaking. She approached me and said, "Hi, I'm Sally, I am the vice president of marketing for Solarity Company." (I've changed her name and the name of her company.) "We are a small marketing and distribution company based here in the Midwest. I am contemplating a move into sales and really appreciated your comments on changing functions."

I haven't seen her since and don't know how successful she was, but she made an impression on me with the clarity and candor of her words and the warmth and confidence she exuded. I'd certainly remember her if she approached me again and reminded me of when we met. The goal is to leave a favorable impression, and the impression is made up of more than words.

Practice delivering your elevator pitch in the mirror. Don't expect it just to come tumbling out of your mouth on the spot. Perfecting your pitch will take some work, but it will be worth it. When you are prepared for an opportunity, you'll find that more and more opportunities will present themselves.

Entry Level

It is never too early to start building your brand. Be known for nailing the basics of business etiquette—promptness, preparedness, and reliability. Even during your personal time, eyes are watching you. When I was 28 and partying with friends at an opening of the Hard Rock Café (at which Oprah and Stedman Graham first stepped out together publicly), I was in a short, revealing dress and ran into a more senior colleague. There were no visible, negative repercussions, but to this day, more than 20 years later, he occasionally mentions that encounter. That is not how I wanted to be remembered.

Mid-Level

To enhance or broaden your reputation within your current company, offer to join employee affinity groups, task forces, and councils where you might meet people from your field. Offer to work on special projects and attend internal seminars to meet people outside of your usual group of colleagues

Executive Level

Don't be overconfident about your brand or your pitch. Constantly refine and clarify the elements of your pitch so it is concise and consistent regardless of audience. You might have become a subject matter expert after years of effort, but recruiters and others will stop calling if you are hard to get along with or don't honor commitments. Don't get blindsided.

Encore Level

Some of the most important sentiments for you to convey in all work settings are adaptability, vitality, technological savvy, and wisdom. These become critical whether you are a part of a cross-generational employee team, a corporate director weighing in on strategy, or an independent consultant seeking new clients.

Detour Route

You can communicate stability and focus even if your road has been rocky. Grouping similar elements from your past when giving examples of key-phrase experiences directs attention to the skill and away from the number of jobs and timeline. Lucy could talk about her experiences in three major categories: retail, restaurant/food services, and, more recently, administrative marketing support. Give the most details in the areas where you are seeking opportunities.

5

THE RÉSUMÉ: YOUR COMPASS FOR CAREER MAPPING

"The best day of your life is the one on which you decide your life is your own. No apologies or excuses. No one to lean on, rely on, or blame. The gift is yours—it is an amazing journey—and you alone are responsible for the quality of it. This is the day your life really begins." ~ Bob Moawad

"I don't see anything on here about you having your own campus radio show, your love of music, or intramural sports," I said to my young coaching client as I glanced over his résumé. "Why isn't any of that on here?"

"Business is business, and my personal life is my personal life," he replied. "I didn't think it was relevant."

"All you are trying to do is connect with people and give them some holistic insight about the person you are," I explained, taking note of the skeptical look on his face. "If you're up for a job against somebody who has the same experience you do, how are you going to make yourself stand out? What makes the difference for an employer? It all comes down to chemistry and connection, and filling in some personal details can have a real impact."

I told him a story about a candidate who was an antique car enthusiast and expressed his passion in a few words at the bottom of his résumé. When I interviewed him for Spencer Stuart, he lit up when I asked him about it. I described his passion for antique cars in the write-up I sent to my client. Unbeknownst to me, my client shared that same passion, and they spent 10 minutes of the interview talking about it. He didn't get the job, but my client had a favorable impression, and he'll likely remember the candidate if something suitable comes up in the future.

You don't always get the perfect happy ending, but part of what you are trying to do is build relationships over time. I said, "Sometimes the linkages come from something seemingly irrelevant. Think of your résumé as a character sketch."

A good résumé shows an employer or executive recruiter where you've been, what you did there, and where you want to go. Although 80-90% of getting a job depends on your skills and experiences, who you are, who you know, what you say in an interview, and what others might say about you, the résumé is the crucial 10-20% of getting a job that secures the interview or meeting in the first place.

Most people think of a résumé as words that provide an outline of your experiences. But employers see it as a collection of data that orients them to a candidate's abilities. Like a real compass, a résumé relies on magnetism to point a would-be employer in the right direction. When I screened résumés as a recruiter, I gave each one an initial look of 3-5 minutes. I was attracted by a few specific key elements. If I didn't see them, I moved on. Here are the key elements:

OBJECTIVE STATEMENT Next to your contact information, which should be at the top and centered, your "objective statement" or "professional profile" is one of the most important pieces of information on your résumé. This is your thesis statement for every résumé you will write. Brevity and conciseness are critical. The objective statement lets the reader know what you are seeking—industries, functions, and roles. Synthesize one of your key focus areas into a 2-4 sentence statement of what you seek and why. Here is an example:

"Marketing director with consumer packaged goods experience seeking to make a transition into industrial sales and marketing role in paper and chemicals industries. Specific expertise in marketing promotions, advertising, and sales management. Led teams up to 30 people; have had extensive leadership development coursework; received company sales leadership awards in 2006, 2008, and 2009."

The Body I love seeing the specificity of people's responsibilities on their résumés. Describe the job, give me a one-liner of what the company does, and tell me about the division in which you work. Why have you been successful in that position?

- **Numbers talk. Use them.** For example, did revenues quadruple during your tenure? How did you contribute?
- **If you want to be a general manager, tell me something about the scale of operations you have worked with so far.** I'm looking for context. Are you better in a startup, turnaround, or a more mature organization? Each requires a different skill set, and your ability to discern that gives me an indication of your self-awareness.
- **Specify what your role was in accomplishing a major task.** Did you lead the team? Were you part of it? What was the time period over which your goal was achieved?
- **Rank your accomplishments in order of importance to you, and be prepared to discuss your rationale for the ranking in an interview.**
- **List degrees in higher education.** If you didn't complete your degree, note the anticipated completion date or say explicitly "degree not conferred" or "coursework completed." Do include dates of graduation—yes, it is often a giveaway for age—but those dates are necessary for verification. Not everyone agrees with this approach, but I feel strongly that applicants should provide this information and that potential employers should verify it.
- **Don't forget to list corporate and not-for-profit board memberships, affiliations with professional associations or civic organizations, and relevant honors and awards.** Don't make this list exhaustive; just list the ones that are current and/or most recognizable.

Some people have been able to have successful careers without ever having written a résumé. They might consider themselves lucky, but if they now need one, they are at a colossal disadvantage. Unless they have kept every old job description and performance review, they likely won't be able to recall or recapture useful information about past roles that would help tell their story to an outside observer. The point is that the résumé is not just your compass to orient a prospective employer to what you can do; it's a chronicle of where you have been—an abbreviated log, journal, ship manifest. Get in the habit of keeping your résumé up to date—whether you think you'll need it or not.

| Permutations of the Theme

CHRONOLOGICAL VS. FUNCTIONAL RÉSUMÉ

Generally, I prefer a chronological résumé, because of the ability to track your trajectory—the pace and logic of your path. When I recruited, functional (skill-based) résumés often frustrated me because functions the person performed got lumped into a heading with no attribution to a specific position; something you did 10 years stional style of résumé provided little in the way of useful context.

Having said that, I am in favor of a hybrid chronological/functional résumé, especially when you are trying to transition from one industry or function to another where you might not have directly relevant experience. For example:

"Marketing director with consumer packaged goods experience seeking to make a transition into industrial sales and marketing role in paper or chemicals industries. Specific expertise in marketing promotions, advertising, and sales management..."

This is a solid objective statement. Embedded in this statement are the three key functional areas where you have expertise and which you will expound upon. You can add up to two more, but do not exceed five. For each of the three functions—marketing promotions, advertising, and sales management—you will honor the same rules for context (the "how") and key words. Keep the detail for each functional description short and sweet because you still have the entire chronological résumé to follow.

For the most significant and relevant jobs you've held, include a short description of your employer or business, no more than 1-2 sentences describing industry, revenues, and geographic scope (local, regional, national, and global). Describe responsibilities in no more than 3-5 brief sentences.

When describing job responsibilities in the chronological section, try not to repeat the same functional examples, but find others that are equally relevant to the position you are seeking. Keep an eye on length because you'll only have the reader's attention for a short time.

Why is the chronological piece so important? Frankly, I form some initial impressions from the speed with which you moved up, over, down, or out. Are you a job hopper, or one who overstayed in a role? Keep in mind that your most recent jobs are generally the most important and relevant, but early information tells a story about you that may yield insights for a skilled reviewer.

For a chronological résumé or the chronological element in a functional résumé, start with the following:

- **List all jobs since graduating from college, most recent roles first.** Go back and edit later; for now, just get it all down.

- Include beginning and end dates (if less than a year, include months).
- Detail all job titles, including special assignments (especially promotions) within the same company.
- Provide the city and state where you were located or the field office where you were based if you worked remotely.

If jobs and responsibilities are too numerous, group them into time periods. Designing a successful résumé is all about showing movement and growth.

RÉSUMÉ ALTERNATIVES

Here are some of my definitions of different career documents and how and when they should be used. They convey very different information and are rarely interchangeable.

BIOGRAPHY This is usually a short (no more than 1-2 pages) narrative about your background featuring mostly what you are doing now. A bio should have color commentary, editorial comments, even quotes from you and others. It's pithy and catchy; think in terms of what you read about speakers at conferences, banquets, or on websites. This is the wallet-size photo version of your background. From a recruiter's or employer's perspective, a bio is a start, but hardly enough to make a full assessment. If you are in a serious job-search mode, get to work on the résumé, because a bio won't be enough.

CURRICULUM VITAE (CV) A CV is a sort of microscopic view of your experience and achievements, with more detail than some might want; I've seen CVs that ran to 30+ pages—ugh! I respect the protocol and attention to detail, but surely not all of those publications, lectures, and awards are of equal importance. Spotlight the most illustrious, recent, and significant, except in academic environments, which place value on every scholarly achievement, piece of research, publication, and speech.

In my experience, CVs often fail to include enough of a chronological work history. If you are an academic making a transition into a non-academic setting, a résumé will be more useful. Depending on the organizations and individuals you are interviewing with, you might have both your CV and your customized résumé on hand.

RÉSUMÉ DO'S AND DON'TS

- Do keep language simple, concise, and professional.
- Do use numbers to help tell the story—budget, people, returns, etc.
- Do assume the reader is well read but not an expert in your field.
- Do make typestyle and formatting readable—no less than 10-point font, no artsy script; use reasonable margins and line spacing.
- Do maintain visual balance to keep the reader's eye moving smoothly.
- Do check your entire document for proper grammar and spelling. Use spelling and grammar checking functions on your computer, but also ask an educated friend to proofread. Relying on spell check can prove tricky if you have an unusual name.
- Don't get tripped up by automatically accepting what the computer tells you. When in doubt, consult your good friends the dictionary and the thesaurus: Thefreedictionary.com or Merriam-Webster.com.
- Don't use acronyms, industry jargon, or buzzwords that don't mean anything to someone outside your field.
- Don't cram everything onto one page. If you have 15 years of experience, allow yourself 1 1/2–2 pages. Anything over three pages is likely to be tedious for a reviewer. Your résumé should be two pages or fewer unless you are a chronic job-hopper or someone with 30 years of must-know-about experience.
- Don't feel compelled to list every responsibility, award, and honor. An interviewer just needs the highlights, not your entire life history.
- Don't get cutesy with fancy paper and pictures. I'll never forget one candidate who enclosed a large glossy photo of herself that looked like it had been taken at Glamour Shots—right down to the seductive pose. Even if you are in creative field, offer a clean résumé or CV that supports your portfolio of work. Do not rely on gimmicks to make yourself memorable; this is not a press kit. You'll be remembered, but not in the way you had hoped.
- Don't forget your contact information—phone numbers, email, mailing address. I know this sounds elementary, but I've seen résumés with just a name.

Dirty Little Secrets

A caveat for those who may have been somewhere or had some problems they would rather not document: Not everyone has a squeaky-clean past. There might be things that you'd rather forget but that people can access in today's information-rich world: that arrest in college for protesting, the litigious neighbor who left suits on your record, a DUI, a nasty article by a reporter. The main thing is to know what's accessible and to be on the offensive about it in case it comes up, either because of a gap in your résumé or a direct question in an interview related to an unflattering aspect of your past.

- Know what is in the public domain about yourself. Start by Googling yourself. Be sure your achievements (positive and negative) won't be mistaken for someone else with the same name.
- On your résumé, use your middle and/or maiden name to distinguish yourself from others with similar names.
- Consider buying a background check on yourself to see what shows up. See sites like Publicrecordfinder.com.
- Have documentation handy that details the resolution of a situation that was not reflected in the public record (e.g., a letter stating case vacated).
- If applications ask about arrests, lawsuits, or any unsavory incidents, answer honestly. The offense itself might not be a deal-breaker, but lying about it will be.

Regardless of your concerns, tell the truth, and be prepared to address any issues an employer or recruiter might want to discuss based on the facts.

Entry Level

Because you lack experience, your résumé should highlight examples of leadership, volunteerism, and coordination skills, including involvement in academic and not-for-profit sectors (e.g., sororities, fraternities, military, Girl Scouts, athletic coaching, and other organizations).

Mid-Level

Your experiences are still light, so describe projects and committee involvement as examples of exposure and responsibility you've had in a relevant function and/or industry. Potential employers love numbers, so quantify your accomplishments. How many people directly report to you, for example?

Executive Level

With the advantage of many years of experience, you have the challenge of sorting through your previous roles with a discerning eye. Consider doing a data dump of accomplishments on a spreadsheet, code them according to the two or three types of résumés you are creating, then sort accordingly to highlight the most relevant activities on each résumé.

Encore Level

Play with a combination of hardcore accomplishments and nuanced experiences that speak to what you want now. Link what you have done to what you love and how you can serve others.

Detour Route

You will be well served by having at least one hybrid résumé that shows both functional expertise and a chronological summary of current and past jobs. You are highlighting what you have done and are good at while lessening the emphasis on where you've worked and the time spent there. The key here is to make your functional categories align with the key functions of the role (or roles) you seek. Pull key words from sample job specifications online.

6

PICKING YOUR CREW

"Friends are as companions on a journey, who ought to aid each other to persevere in the road to a happier life." ~ Pythagoras

We have been building a methodology for managing your career and finding the best job for you at this stage in your journey. Remember that what I am showing you is a process, which means it has a sequence: a beginning, middle, and end. I have designed this process to be used repeatedly throughout your working life. I would suggest making an assessment using your career map at least annually—even when you feel satisfied in your current role.

So far, we've covered:

- Getting your head straight about where you are; examining who you are and why you are here (Chapter 1).
- Plotting your past job history, creating job prototypes, and mapping your aspirational jobs by identifying industries, companies, roles, and titles. This is crucial. Go back and review if need be (Chapter 2).
- Conducting a personal inventory involving a deep assessment of your skills, wants, and needs (Chapter 3).
- Communicating the elements of your personal brand and perfecting
  your elevator pitch with language gathered from the plotting process (Chapter 4).
- Creating your customized résumés to speak to each role for which you want to be considered based on your career map (Chapter 5).

Before we move on, take a little time to go back and review each of these important steps on your career map. In the next phase I will coach you on the fine art of networking—or "network mapping." Straightforward but not always easy to execute, network mapping requires that you do your preparatory work. Get ready!

Many people view networking as cheap self-promotion or as seeking disingenuous alliances. Done poorly, it can be those things. Done well, it offers great benefits not just for finding a job, but for gaining essential career insights and identifying business opportunities. Here are but a few of the benefits:

- Exposure to job opportunities and introductions to job influencers.
- Valued perceptions of your current skills, gaps, and attributes through the eyes of others.
- Advice on how to advance or effectively maneuver in your current position.
- Perspective on whether your goals and expectations are realistic.
- References and recommendations that support your pursuit of new opportunities.

I will help you think through each and every type of person who needs to be on your list: why they are on the list, what you need to ask of them, and how you need to approach them to build lasting, productive relationships.

| Relationship Building

After getting that business card at the reception, but before sending out the email or placing the phone call to invite the person to lunch or coffee, you consider, sometimes unconsciously, what it is you want from this relationship—what's the motive? After some form of ongoing contact, you assess other dynamics between you to know whether this relationship is productive, enjoyable, and something you want to invest in.

Here are the elements that will determine if this person becomes part of your network or remains a passing acquaintance:

MOTIVE What you both want out of this relationship is often expressed explicitly; e.g., "I would like to learn more about your industry/company as I am contemplating a job move." Initially you might not know what either of you wants, or you might have an implicit, unexpressed reason for wanting to know one another, but over time a motive—good, bad, or otherwise—will emerge.

AUTHENTICITY Here is that word again. We used it in the branding section, and it is equally important when building relationships. The ability to be yourself with someone is as important in professional relationships as it is in personal ones. Consider an interview with a potential boss in which you just don't feel like you can express your real opinions or act naturally. Big problem.

TRUST This ingredient is fundamental to business relationships. Your ability to keep confidences is as important as others keeping yours. You also want to trust someone to give you honest and objective opinions or insight and to be equally open to receiving it from you. That's trust.

RECIPROCITY Relationships can't be one-way. Remember the Golden Rule ("Do unto others…"), and be considerate of people's time. Never assume you have nothing to give someone in return for their generosity.

RESPECT You don't have to like me, but you must respect me. In the workplace it is about business first, possible friendships later. Respect is earned by doing your job well and demonstrating integrity; expect it from yourself and others.

SUSTAINABILITY As in personal relationships, you must make an investment in professional relationships in order to sustain them. Enduring connections come from making regular contact—even when you don't need anything.

| Defining Your Network

One of the biggest holes I recognize in most people's career maps appears in the area of network definition. Most people define their networks—if they've given any thought at all to this important piece—far too narrowly. Even the people who have paid attention to their networks over the years often make the mistake of focusing on just one or two of the types of people who should make up an active and supportive network. Here is who should be on your radar:

REFERENCES People with whom you have worked closely in the last five years who can attest to specific professional competencies. A full list will include superiors, subordinates, and peers.

- Contact references in advance to make sure they are comfortable speaking about you in detail.
- Advise them on what to say about you. By that I mean let them know about the position so they can tailor their comments accordingly.
- When possible, let your references know the name, company, and title of the person (or people) who might be contacting them so they can respond quickly.
- Determine their preferred means of contact (phone or email).
- When you are giving a reference for someone, be as specific as possible about how the person performs or performed. Give examples. Don't recite their résumé and work history; the caller already knows that information.

CO-WORKERS These are people with whom you work or have worked (regardless of function) and whom you know well enough to ask a favor of. They are acquaintances with whom you share (or shared) a common employer. Cultivating relationships with these people can give you access, leads, and/or insight. Not sure who to get to know in this category? Here are some ideas:

- Consider reaching out to someone you went through a training class with but don't work with everyday.
- Get to know people in groups or functions within your company that you might have an interest in moving into or want to learn more about.
- Participate in affinity groups or community-oriented events with co-workers as a way to increase visibility and find out about different opportunities within the company.
- Reach out to people who might benefit from knowing you, especially younger, more junior colleagues. Don't just build relationships up the food chain; you need to know people at all levels in your world. You never know when that executive assistant or research analyst can help you out of a tight spot. Their willingness to help might be because of a relationship you've forged, not because of rank.

ADVISORS, MENTORS, AND SPONSORS These are usually people who have insight or expertise that is relevant to the job, company, or industry you seek to learn more about. They know you well professionally and personally and can give honest, unfiltered feedback (to you and others) on your performance, presentation style, and more. Stick to asking advisors, mentors, and sponsors pointed questions or for advice on job strategies, specific companies, and the like.

Don't overlook contacts with the competition, especially if they are more seasoned and senior than you. As long as you aren't sharing company secrets, you can learn much about your industry from these folks.

When I first started at Spencer Stuart, I was not used to business development in a professional services environment, having just come from the world of commercial real estate. I reached out to an acquaintance who happened to be a partner at a competing firm. A year earlier, despite an introductory call placed by a mutual friend, he had not returned my phone call when I reached out to explore possibilities with his firm. Given my new role, this time he was responsive.

We held quarterly meetings in which he coached me and shared some of his secrets for development in the executive search business. What was in it for him? He gained perspective on how his competition was on-boarding people. There were certainly no company secrets for either of us to share. I think helping me appealed to his altruistic nature. At the time I was hired, I joined him as one of fewer than 20 African Americans in senior-level executive search firms. For the first year and a half of my time with Spencer Stuart, this man coached me.

We stayed in touch in the ensuing 10 years while I was at Spencer Stuart, and I reached out to him after starting my consulting business. Once again he took the time to understand the scope of my offerings. Three months later he recommended me for some consulting work that was out of his firm's scope. Thanks to staying in touch, I landed a three-month, five-figure consulting engagement with his client. We both won: He looks good with his longstanding client, and I got consulting work.

Incidentally, if I begrudged him that initial failure to respond, I would have missed out on a powerful mentor.

- For a good *mentor*, consider a person at least one level higher than you and someone you don't report to. Don't wait for formal programs; find your own mentor based on a mutual vibe you have with that person—and their willingness and accessibility.
- Your current boss may be a great *sponsor*, but only after you've proven you are worthy of him/her going out on a limb for you.
- Former (or current) professors can be great *advisors*, since they know some of your intellectual capabilities and possible tendencies; they can give great feedback as to how well suited you might be for a role or industry. Keep in mind, academics at the top of the heap often do consulting work with businesses and have excellent contacts and current, valuable insights.

INDUSTRY AND FUNCTIONAL EXPERTS You don't have to know these people, but you can solicit their advice with targeted questions about how they see the current and future prospects for the industry and/or function. They may even be able to offer opinions on or insights into some of your targeted companies. These people are especially valuable when you are trying to break into an industry or function you haven't worked in previously.

One year out of business school, I decided I didn't like the credit/lending aspect of banking, but I liked the real estate aspect of what I was doing. I didn't know much about the real estate industry, so I researched the top local companies in leasing, property management, and development. This was before the Internet was popular, so I had to leaf through industry magazines and ask people I knew for leads.

I identified half a dozen people I wanted to get to know and learn from. I cold-called them and asked for a 20-minute meeting, for which I had a clear agenda. Over the course of six months, I got to everyone on my list and learned enough to decide where I wanted to go. I joined LaSalle Partners (now Jones Lang LaSalle) less than a year later in an asset management role. One of the contacts I had made introduced me to the person that eventually hired me.

I stayed with the firm for four years and was in the industry for nearly 10 years before moving to executive search. The point is, ask people to share their professional insights with you, tell people what your objectives are, be purposeful, and create opportunities for yourself. **HERE ARE SOME TIPS:**

- Research and identify the most respected and senior people you think you can access.
- Though you are on a fact-finding mission, you are making an impression—present yourself accordingly.
- Prepare targeted questions specifically related to what the individual does to show you've done your homework and are respectful of that person's time.
- During the meeting, honor the other person's time limitations and don't overstay your welcome.
- Show your gratitude and offer to reciprocate. You might think you don't have much to offer, but even being willing to edit or review a pet project or sending a pair of sports tickets is an appreciated gesture.
- Don't lead with your résumé; leave it behind, or send as an attachment with the thank-you email or note.

FRIENDS People you trust who can give you honest feedback about how you present yourself in different settings. While not always unbiased, friends can tell you the good and the bad about yourself.

- Get an honest assessment of your image from a good friend. Is that hairstyle from high school really still working for you? Does that suit from 20 lbs. ago still flatter you? Are you projecting the maturity and professionalism you want to project?
- Ask a friend to conduct a mock interview with you or listen to your elevator pitch.
- Have your friends check your speech patterns (volume, pitch, extraneous words) and hand gestures when presenting in a one-on-one or group setting. In Chapter 4 we discussed this in relation to image. It is very important.
- Tell your friends what you are seeking from your career or in your job search—you don't know everyone they know.
- Be a friend to your friends and offer constructive feedback to them (when asked). It increases your chances of receiving the same.

ALUMNI NETWORK This can be a rich network that should be cultivated throughout your professional life. Social networking has made it so easy to identify and reach classmates from college, graduate school, and even high school. You've got nothing to lose and everything to gain by staying in touch with people.

A year ago, while traveling on vacation in London, I got a LinkedIn acceptance to an invitation I had sent to a Kellogg classmate weeks earlier. He was a fellow executive recruiter with another firm, and he was congratulating me on my transition from search. He suggested we connect to compare notes, saying he'd be in Chicago in the fall, but that I should get in touch if I was in London. It was my last day in London.

I immediately sent him a note saying I happened to be in London for one more day, and I asked if there was any chance he was free for lunch. He was! We had the most inspiring and fruitful conversation, and we will surely be working on a project together in the future. I had not seen this man in 25 years, but since we reconnected over our shared alma mater via the Internet, we have seen each other to discuss this book and his own book project.

- Periodically attend alumni networking events in your city. If you are a subject matter expert, offer to be a speaker.
- In addition to leveraging the career management center, you can tap into the usually secure alumni website (with your password) to find former classmates who are working or have worked in your space. Occasionally you will even find job postings from employers.
- Go to reunions. Get on the planning committee and leverage your own network for the benefit of your whole class. I was amazed at the number of who people attended my 25-year reunion and how many people remembered me and wanted to help me with my new undertaking.
- Send updates to the alumni newsletter, which provides an easy way to help people find you.
- "Alumni" do not have to be limited to just graduates of academic institutions. Many large corporations have formed alumni networks expressly for the purpose of providing former employees a forum in which they can share information. Again, social networks (like LinkedIn and Facebook) have such groups and are easy to join. One of the coolest aspects of networking on the web is that you can connect with people you have never worked with or even met! Common experience breeds familiarity.

EXECUTIVE RECRUITERS Having been an executive recruiter for 12 years with one of the world's leading firms, I feel strongly that job seekers should *not* expect recruiters to hold the key to their next opportunity. Recruiters are intermediaries who work for the employer, and while they are aware of many excellent opportunities, those opportunities represent a relatively small fraction of all the jobs hired for in any given year.

I would even suggest that in difficult economic times, employers forgo paying the executive recruiter's hefty fees in favor of posting internally or doing the search themselves. Having said that, there is an art to knowing how to deal with search firms so that you *do* get the call when they have something juicy:

- Identify the firms that work in your current or intended industry and function.
- Recognize these names and return the calls you receive from these firms.

- **If you aren't interested in what they are calling about, tell them what you *are* interested in.** Refer or recommend others you know who might be right for the role. Recruiters make note of that in your record and will keep calling you if you are helpful and cooperative.
- **When seeking a contact at a firm, determine the search consultants who work in your field and send your résumé to them electronically to upload into their database.** Their names are on the firms' websites. Do not write a "Dear Recruiter" cover letter!
- **Request a "courtesy interview" to get to know the specific search consultants so they have a feel for how you present yourself—even if they don't have a client with a current need for someone with your background.**
- **Don't stalk recruiters to see if they "have anything."** Focus your energy and time on executing your own career mapping strategy.
- **See Chapter 8 for more on executive recruiters.**

SOCIAL MEDIA LinkedIn, Facebook, Twitter, MySpace, and other social networking sites are places you can express your job interests and get leads. Note that confidentiality generally goes out the window in these situations, so be judicious. I'm a big LinkedIn fan and have more than 1,300 contacts (and counting). This site is a great way to stay abreast of people's professional movement and to reach out to assist, ask a favor, or cheer them on. On LinkedIn you can see how many degrees separate you from someone you might want to know, and you can see who knows the person you want to contact.

On Facebook I reached out to an author by whom I was hugely impressed after seeing him speak on Ted.com. He responded and invited me as a friend. I don't *need* anything from him apart from the fact that I want him to know who I am, and I want to be "in his orbit"—and for him to be in mine. So yes, when you have an objective (as part of a larger strategy), these sites can be great ways to identify, keep track of, and connect with people.

I will keep reiterating the need for a clear strategy before casting the wide net that creates your network. Have your plan and stay focused on what and who you need to know. Invest the most time on those people who can do the most for you, and don't get distracted by the dazzle and buzz of social media.

A Simple "Hello" Will Do

I was talking to a friend who is a VP of human resources. We work out at the same health club, and we were talking about how shocking it is when people with whom you establish eye contact—and to whom you might even say hello because you've seen them every other day at 6 a.m. for five years running—can't bring themselves to smile, much less say hello. She mentioned the name of someone I know who behaves this way. I happened to know this person has been out of work. Wouldn't you think someone in job-search mode would be completely gracious, respectful, and outgoing as often as possible?

You never know when you are encountering someone who might be in a position to help you professionally. You simply can't afford to judge people based on appearances, especially when you are not in a professional or business setting; that means at the car wash, health club, grocery store, or on an elevator.

When I worked as a recruiter, I can't tell you how many times I'd ride the elevator up to my office (especially after lunch) and guess which person was the candidate I was about to interview. I noted whether the candidate initiated, responded to, or rejected eye contact with me, and I quickly formed a positive or negative impression of the person. Our minds work that way. Don't be foolish; offer that passing glance with a twinkle in your eye, or spring for a full-blown hello. Being warm and friendly doesn't cost a thing—but being unfriendly can potentially cost you a job!

| Leveraging the Network

We started out talking about networking, and I hope you've found the detailed commentary on every type of contact in your network helpful. Now the real work begins: You have to effectively utilize these people to get what you need. I spoke with a mentee recently who was very excited to have gotten several meetings and interviews set up with a variety of companies for prospective job opportunities. His wonderful personality makes getting meetings easy for him. He rattled off four different functional roles in three different industries. I stopped him there.

"What are you doing?" I asked. "Where's the focus? I can't believe you are going to be compelling to any one of these people you are meeting with since you've not committed to any one (or two) functional roles, much less one or two industries. You're all over the map!"

He said, "Oh, I guess you're right. I was so happy to get the meetings, I wasn't focused on how the roles might really enhance my career."

So here's the advice:
- **Before you contact any member of your network, start with your career map, your overall strategy of where you are trying to go.** The strategy can and will change as you get more information from all sources, including your network, but you need a starting point.
- **If you are looking for a job, determine which people from your network can give you access to people at your targeted companies—preferably people at the senior levels.**
- **If you are looking to broaden your network for future opportunities, technical advice, or career enhancement, be strategic about the people you seek out.**
- **Approach people with a clear agenda in mind, and *don't waste their time!*** Have your four or five questions ready, and then listen well.
- **Record notes after every meeting detailing the advice, resources, names, and next steps.**
- **Send a thank-you note acknowledging the time the person took to meet with you.**

| Generosity and Reciprocity

Networking is an art that is nuanced. People who do it best understand unspoken rules and demonstrate generosity, reciprocity, and respect. When I was an executive recruiter, I was always popular at parties. (And I like to think I still am!) People would sidle up to me and say (sometimes in a whisper) that they wanted to send me their résumés.

No problem. I'm in the service business and genuinely want to help people. I would gladly add these people to the firm's database and my own contacts list. Invariably, though, I would find people who would not return my occasional phone call, but when they needed a job or career advice, they would pursue me relentlessly and without regard for the value of my time.

Peter Shankman, author, public relations expert, and master networker, recently took a blogger to task for daring to challenge him on this last point. Here's how his very public exchange went, played out before the 130,000 people who subscribe to his blog, HelpAReporter.com, and his 88,300 Twitter followers:

Email me—I tell people every day. Got a quick question? Happy to answer it. I put my damn cell phone number in the sigfile of every email I write. There's a big difference between "Peter, would you use Facebook or Twitter to reach teenagers?" and "Peter, I'd like you to do six hours of work for me for free in exchange for a hot dog, and it won't be considered work, because I call it 'picking your brain' and it sounds much nicer that way!"

Within a few hours, Kami Watson Huyse, APR, wrote a blog post telling the world that my tweet (saying "picking my brain" would now cost $400 an hour) was a pet peeve of hers. She believes I've gotten too famous for my own good.

Peter's response:

Kami: I'd like to take you to lunch. I have no intention of paying for said lunch (we can go Dutch!). But I'd like to get at least an hour to sit down with you, probably closer to two hours. During that time, I'd like to show you (and make you read) my business plan for my new startup. I'd also like you to not only comment on it, but tell me what exactly I should do in the marketing section of it. I'll need it back by Thursday, but you're welcome to take it home and send it back to me by email as long as it gets to me by Thursday.

Once you do that, I was wondering if I could call you or email you at least once a week with another question. I know that you consult to Fortune 100 companies and give them the same advice I'm asking for, for lots and lots of money, but I'm asking you to do it for me, multiple times, for free. You're nice, so I know you'll say yes, right?

That sound good?

If you don't get it to me in time, I'll probably just email you every few days to see how it's going, then start calling you on your mobile. Maybe even at home.

So—Yeah—If you could get that all to me (did I mention for free? I did, right?) that'd be great.

OK? Thanks.

You're so awesome,

-Peter

PS: A good friend of a friend of mine is looking for a job. Any chance you're hiring? I've included her résumé, and also given her your phone number so she can call you directly. Thanks again, you're a peach!

So, Kami, does my tweet make a little more sense now? Feel free to call me—Let's have lunch and talk about it. I'll even pay.

Indeed, there are givers and takers in this world. I'm generally a giver and will give to takers—but only to a point. There is the rule of reciprocity that comes into play. It's not about keeping score, but you must realize that when things are one-way, they aren't sustainable.

If you consciously choose to be generous to others, you will always be in a position to ask the occasional favor. Here are a few tips on how to make sure you are striking the right give/take balance. All of these suggestions are great not only for keeping in touch with your existing contacts list, but also for cultivating new contacts and developing new business. *Givers get and takers drain.* Which will you be?

- Invite (and pay for) clients and contacts to attend seminars or luncheons to hear speakers you think they would find interesting.
- **Invest time in people who show curiosity, promise, and gratitude; they can inspire your thinking.** Be generous with your time, but set boundaries.
- **While waiting in airports, run through your contacts and pop off 5-10 emails to people you haven't talked to in six months or more.** People love to be thought about when you clearly have no agenda.
- **Send articles that are of interest to people on your contacts list to let them know you are thinking about them.**
- **If you hear of or read about a contact's personal triumph (promotion, marriage, birth, etc.) or tragedy (death, illness, etc.), fire off a handwritten card or note, or send flowers to express your sentiments.** People remember kindness and consideration.

Entry Level

Since you have the fewest years out of college, stay close to fellow alumni. Though the people you know best are generally your same age and level, everyone is building a network of increasingly senior and influential people you can all share. Don't hesitate to reach out to the alumni who are more senior; they may be looking to hire and mentor more junior fellow classmates.

Mid-Level

To fortify your list of external contacts, start attending conferences and association meetings. Stick with the ones that are relevant to your job so you can get the company to pick up the tab, but consider footing the bill for those that expose you to the biggest names in your field. Have your elevator pitch honed and ready, your business cards in hand, and go forth and conquer!

Executive Level

Knowing a lot of people isn't the same as having a robust network. Stay active in civic and cultural organizations and professional associations so people can see you in action. This way people are actually recommending you for having done good work, not just referring you as a name on a list of acquaintances.

Encore Level

Even if you are approaching retirement or downshifting to a lower profile, stay in touch with people across generations to stay current on all aspects of business and culture. This ensures that you will continue to be valued as a great businessperson, board director, grandparent, and person in general.

Detour Route

If you have hopscotched across industries and functions or have fallen out of touch with people, don't be afraid to reconnect. People are generally kind and want to help, even if they are not directly related to what you might want to do. It is critically important that you to approach everyone in your network with clear and consistent objectives.

FINDING YOUR WAY

"THE FUTURE BELONGS TO THOSE WHO BELIEVE IN THE BEAUTY OF THEIR DREAMS."
- ELEANOR ROOSEVELT

7

BY LAND: THE DIRECT APPROACH

"If one advances confidently in the direction of his dreams, and endeavors to live the life which he has imagined, he will meet with success unexpected in common hours." ~ Henry David Thoreau

| Exclusive Access

The whole point of career mapping is that you take yourself through a disciplined regimen to determine what you want to do, what you are capable of doing, and where you want to do it. You have consciously chosen specific companies where you believe you can be valued and satisfied. We have been funneling information down into this intricate flow that will result in the job you want. You won't be pulled into the vortex if you stay on course and steer yourself carefully to your next destination.

This is where the rubber meets the road, where the wind hits the sails—whatever you like. You have your map, you've checked all the gauges, and you've assembled the crew. This is what you have been waiting for: access to that all-important contact at your target company. These are the encounters that will test your resolve and your patience, but fear not; you are not alone, and you are well-prepared.

| Ports of Entry

You are going to deploy artfully that crew you enlisted in the last chapter and watch the ports open. Here are a few things to keep in mind as you rev the engines for the approach:

An acquaintance named Matt sent me an email not long ago asking if I would "clear the way" for him. He had applied for an opportunity at a company I worked for many years ago but where I maintain some senior-level contacts. These contacts have been clients, former colleagues, and there is at least one fellow not-for-profit board member. How did this man that I've only known a year know that? He checked LinkedIn and it showed people in his network (namely, me) who were linked to the hiring managers for the role he sought.

Matt sent me the position specification and his résumé as part of his request. He had been in the executive search business, and he and I were working on a project together that he continued to work on as a freelance marketing professional. I had never seen his résumé, so I reviewed it and compared it to the position description for the job he sought. He met the requirements, and I felt comfortable recommending him. I posed a few questions to clarify some points on his résumé, and he made a few revisions. I was being careful because I was recommending him for consideration based only on limited interaction. My reputation was at stake, and I knew Matt knew that. I did forward his résumé to my most senior contact, and within a day one of her subordinates called me to say he had received the information and would review it.

A few days later Matt sent me an email telling me he had an interview scheduled and would keep me posted. Soon after that he followed up, saying that the job went to someone who had industry experience he did not have, but he was appreciative of my assistance. Despite not getting the job, Matt had a successful approach. He leveraged his network beautifully by asking me to assist with a specific role for which he was qualified.

It's not likely that I will approach my contacts at that company with any other favors anytime soon, but my credibility remains intact even though Matt wasn't the successful candidate. Similarly, it's not likely that Matt will ask me for anything again soon so as not to wear out his welcome. I received notice about a month later that Matt secured a marketing role with a law firm. He expanded and nurtured his network effectively.

| Time Management

Embarking on a career journey is not an invitation to drift and see where you wash up. Other people are investing time in your search and fueling your journey. You may be captain of the ship, but the sails must be up to catch the wind.

A friend recently told me of a pro bono consulting assignment he was doing for a not-for-profit. He was involved in the cause and hoped that networking with some of the organization's board members would present career opportunities. He was, after all, "in transition" and actively looking for a new role or consulting assignment—paid, that is.

He admitted that he had spent most of his time during the preceding week on this pro bono assignment, except for several hours during which he interviewed for one possible opportunity. That is fine—if and only if you keep up with the structured strategy you are working on to execute your career change or job search.

You need to suit up and show up for the "housekeeping tasks," as well as for the big networking events that you think "might" do you some good. Do not get trapped in the shallow water of "giving" your talents away or in dizzying whirlpools of nonproductive activity.

- **Keep up your three-ring binder or database of all your company or business development targets, networking contacts, contact notes, and action steps.** Try to add to it every day.
- **If you're not adding to your base, you should be following up on every possibility, reaching out to people in your network weekly or daily.** Remember, you are not looking just for posted openings. You are introducing yourself for future reference.
- **Start your day doing the thing you least like to do—the one thing that usually falls to the bottom of the list.**
- **Forgive yourself if you don't do that thing the first couple times.** The third time, ask yourself if this is something you should be doing. Why the blockage? See a job or life coach, even a therapist, if you can't follow through on your plans.
- **Execute consistently, and be honest with yourself.** If you are not performing well for yourself, what makes you think you can convince an employer of your productivity? Address your issues

so that you come across to contacts as a valuable asset who knows your own worth.

| Deviations from the Course

We all take jobs for specific reasons: to pay the rent, something to do until school starts, to get your footing in a new location—the list is long. However, once you are no longer just holding a series of jobs and instead have a bona fide career, you need a sound rationale for taking the next job. Usually the driving force is desire for greater responsibility, skill-building, greater compensation, ability to relocate, or even working for a certain talented person with whom you might have worked previously. The presumption is that because you've had a good working relationship with this person, he/she has your best interests at heart and will be in a position to offer you continued professional growth and relative security. The sense of loyalty is comforting, and you, in turn, are compelled to do your best work for him/her.

I've watched people make this practice a pattern, and they usually follow a boss from one organization to the next. It can work well until your boss leaves, no longer values or has use for your skills, or, worst of all, you wake up to find you aren't growing—you've effectively been used. Family members in family-owned businesses run this risk, usually with far more complications. You can end up with an assortment of unrelated jobs and skills that don't hang together and will make it hard to move into your next role. You can really compromise what could have been a good professional relationship by hitching your wagon to others and making them responsible for your success.

- **Don't allow yourself to become a "utility player."** While it can be flattering to be asked to perform several functions, and it can even be skill-enhancing, you are at risk of becoming a "jack of all trades, but master of none."
- **Accept only positions with clearly articulated responsibilities, a job description, success measures, and some understanding of your next logical role;** make sure it fits with your longer-term career strategy.

- Be dubious of any opportunity based on friendship, loyalty, or a sense of obligation—the only person you owe anything to is yourself (and maybe the IRS!).
- Adopt the free-agency mindset that says you know what your transferable skills are and what you are worth.
- No one is responsible for your professional success but you!

Entry Level

You will likely have more degrees of separation between yourself and points of entry, so you must leverage every possible means of introduction, including responding to job postings for target companies, sending unsolicited emails to human resources executives, attending job fairs, following target companies on Twitter and LinkedIn, and more.

Mid-Level

You might have more personal contacts, but you will still need to be resourceful, especially if you are shifting gears to another industry or function. For example, go aggressively after warm leads generated at networking and industry conferences. Focus on crafting a concise and effective approach that gets attention.

Executive Level

You are seeking the most senior points of entry possible—ideally through personal contacts with the fewest degrees of separation. Focus on creating only the highest-quality opportunities possible (e.g., the most lucrative or senior positions, best location, and the like) for your area of expertise. Think quality over quantity.

Encore Level

If you are moving to another field, you might have to resort to some tactics from earlier in your career, but your advantage lies in knowing how to leverage both your existing base of contacts and your seasoned approach. Be sure you are up to date with your technological skills, and make effective use of online social and professional networking sites, which have emerged as vital tools for identifying possible opportunities.

Detour Route

Don't be afraid to approach companies for a role they don't yet have or for a role for which you aren't exactly qualified. You could be just the person to fill a role they have been thinking about or that has arisen because of an acquisition, crisis, or new line of business. Do your homework to find out about situations in which you can add value. The onus is on you to tell them!

8

BY SEA: ALTERNATE ROUTES

"It is our choices that show what we truly are, far more than our abilities." ~ J. K. Rowling

| Executive Recruiters and Other Intermediaries

Intermediaries get bad reputations and are sometimes lumped into the same parasitic category as used car salesmen. But pay attention: Not all intermediaries are created equal. Remember that only a fraction of all hires are made through intermediaries like recruiters; at least 80% of all jobs are filled through networking, which we discussed in the previous chapters.

There are several types of companies that act as intermediaries by facilitating the placement of people in new positions. In a somewhat oversimplified view, they tend to be stratified according to the level of the role one is seeking:

- Employment agencies generally find hourly workers, administrative assistants, etc.
- Placement agencies take a fee from the person seeking employment and attempt to shop the person around to prospective employers, sort of like sports, literary, or other talent agents.
- Outplacement firms are usually retained by employers to work with former employees—usually executives—who recently have been let go (except those who were let go with cause). These firms help the "outplaced" person with self-assessment, résumé preparation, and even present the individual to recruiters.
- Executive search firms tend to work in specific industries—like manufacturing, financial services, health services, and real estate—or functions—like operations, information technol-

ogy, and finance—and at specific levels, usually delineated by compensation.

Sometimes revered, other times despised, recruiters and the roles they play in careers remain mysterious to and misunderstood by most. If you have never worked with an executive recruiter—or even if you have—this is when I pull back the curtain to reveal exactly how the process works and what you need to know.

There are two types of executive search firms: those that are contingent and those that are retained. Both contingency and retained firms typically charge 1/3 of the placement's first-year cash compensation (base salary plus anticipated or targeted bonus). However, today's competitive market has brought with it a widespread reduction in the fees firms are able to command for their services.

- **The contingency firms get paid by the employer only if the person they introduce is hired by the employer—the fee is contingent upon the hire.** Many contingency firms work at lower- to mid-management levels. They are sometimes more aggressive in sending out résumés to increase the chances of a hire. They often work with companies on high-volume hires; for example, they might recruit 50-100 sales associates at a time for a single company.
- **Retained firms work like a law firm in that they earn their fee regardless of the outcome of the assignment.** The reputation of the recruiter is at stake, so recruiters are committed to finding candidates well suited to the placement. Among the top firms, the placement rate is around 80%. (There are many reasons that account for the other 20%, including searches being cancelled before they're filled.) Retained firms generally get the most senior searches and have longstanding relationships with companies. They benefit from knowing specific details about the company's people, culture, and business issues.

Most of the largest firms are retained, and they have specialists in numerous industry and functional areas. The largest search firms cover all the major industries—financial services, industrial, education/not-for-profit, life sciences, etc.—and have functional practices in, for example, chief marketing officers, chief technology/information officers, financial officers, and human resources. Their consultants (the recruiters) often come from industry; contrary to the popular belief that they are trained in human resources, most recruiters have worked in roles similar to the ones they recruit for. This makes them knowledgeable about the industry or function, able to leverage personal contacts, and gives them credibility with clients (the employers) and the suitable candidates they identify.

Executive recruiters are brokers at worst, consultants at best. Granted, they get a bad reputation because they don't always return job seekers' calls. They are also accused by companies of presenting pricier people to drive the fee up. I have, in fact, had some acquaintances in the profession (whose integrity I question) who were known to show clients people who were clearly not qualified as a "stalling" tactic. I won't dwell on the few bad examples of the broader profession, but suffice to say that you, the candidate, should be mindful of the reputation and motives of the search firm you are working with.

The main thing to remember is that search firms' first allegiance is to the employers who hired them to find candidates. The likelihood that they will have an opportunity that suits your background right now is slim unless you are at a senior level—but that doesn't mean that they aren't worth exploring.

Even if an executive recruiter doesn't currently have a client who needs your skill set, recruiters can absolutely be helpful in providing perspective and facilitating useful connections. Here are some frequently asked questions, the responses to which offer critical pieces of the puzzle that must be in place before you contact or respond to a recruiter:

HOW DO I KNOW WHICH RECRUITERS I CAN TRUST WITH MY CAREER? Honestly, the only person you can trust with your career is you. While you might establish good relationships with certain recruiters, the relationship is largely transactional. Your favorite recruiters are genuinely looking out for you, but the opportunities they present to you are what their clients are hiring them to fill. If you are actively looking to make a transition, you must establish your own strategy, of which recruiters will be a part. Nevertheless, here are some ways to screen recruiters:

- If a recruiter contacts you, check the company website and the bio of the consultant who called to get a sense of their experience, specialty, and reputation.
- Google recruiters to see, for example, if they speak at industry conferences or have written articles or books that suggest an investment in thought leadership.
- If it was a more junior associate who called, return the call; if you are sincerely interested in the opportunity, request that the lead consultant call you. Here are a few questions to ask: *How long have they been in search?*

  What were they doing before? (Many worked in the industry they now recruit for.)

  Who are some of their recent clients? Who are some recent placements, and what were the positions in which they were placed?

  Are there client and/or placement references you can talk to?

- If you are seeking out a few recruiters you want to make yourself known to, identify the firms that work in your space and the names of the consultants who specialize in your function. Check out the Association of Executive Search Consultants (AESC.org) or the Online Recruiters Directory (Onlinerecruitersdirectory.com) to get some names of firms you might want to contact.
- Ask successful executives in your space who are at your level or are more senior which recruiters call them and how responsive and trustworthy they are. Industry conferences are a good place to do this.
- Good recruiters will make time for you when you have the occasional career question. Recruiters are not placement agents, but they want to see executives (even if they are not current candidates) make good career decisions. They can provide valuable insight into specific companies and connect you with other executives you might end up working with. If you need a longer-term plan, consult a career or executive coach.

I OFTEN GET CALLS FROM EXECUTIVE RECRUITERS, BUT I'M NOT INTERESTED IN CHANGING JOBS, SO I IGNORE THE CALLS. AM I MISSING SOMETHING?

Put simply, yes, you are. Most of the people recruiters place are not seeking new opportunities and are performing well in their current roles. Keep an open mind. Figure out which firms/boutiques are most actively recruiting in your industry or function; know the top five firms if you have a national/global platform (Korn/Ferry, Heidrick & Struggles, Spencer Stuart, Russell Reynolds, and Egon Zehnder, in the executive search world). Try to get to know the names of the consultants/partners in those practice areas, and call them back when they reach out to you. Here's why:

- **Get on the radar; tell the recruiter what would get you interested: when, where, and how much.** Send your résumé to keep on file. Good recruiters keep your confidence.
- **Even if you aren't interested, you can assist recruiters by referring or recommending people you might know (confidentially, if need be).** Recruiters make notes (literally) of your cooperation (or lack thereof) and will call again (or not) based in part on these notes.
- **Your willingness to cooperate fosters goodwill, and they will call you when they have an opportunity that suits your background and interests.**
- **It's a chance for you to ask about trends the recruiters are seeing in the market and to get a sense of your marketability and value.**
- **You are in a position to gauge the professionalism and knowledge of recruiters and decide if you would ever want to use them for a search need you might have.**
- **This is a chance for you to practice your pitch to a discerning listener.** Ask for feedback on your comments—after all, part of this is about you building your brand.

Entry Level

You should not invest money in agencies or sites that promise to find you a job. With the tools I have helped you develop through the career mapping and networking processes, you are ready for your own approach to your target companies. You can also make excellent use of many of the free online resources; for instance, upload your résumé to job search sites (Monster.com, CareerBuilder.com, and TheLadders.com, to name a few).

Mid-Level

You need to get on the radars of the search firms that work in your area. Upload your résumé to the sites of the most well-known firms and/or send a targeted email (with your résumé attached) to the recruiters in your function or industry. Ask for an acknowledgment of receipt, but don't expect to get a call back or a meeting every time.

Executive Level

You should be getting periodic (if not regular) calls from search firms. Solidify your relationships with a handful of individual recruiters at these firms by returning their calls promptly every time and by offering candidate leads, even if you are not interested in or qualified for what they are calling about. This responsiveness almost guarantees that you will get the call when they have something that really will pique your interest.

Encore Level

Recruiters can help you indirectly in the process of identifying opportunities for a transition from your traditional role to a new vocation or avocation by providing a wealth of information and leads related to trends and new ports of entry you might not have considered.

Detour Route

If you have been out of work, you are probably at a disadvantage compared to others in the qualified pool, because recruiters are paid to find people who are currently doing what their client needs done. That doesn't, however, mean you shouldn't let recruiters know what kinds of industries, functions, and roles you are seeking. The more specific you are, the more likely recruiters are to be able to help you, but be careful not to develop a dependency. Make recruiters a part of your network, not your primary job-hunting strategy.

9

 NAVIGATING THE INTERVIEW

"One can never consent to creep when one feels an impulse to soar." ~ Helen Keller

After I graduated from the University of California, Davis, I worked for the university as a college recruiter. I recall always being impressed with the students who had a sense of clarity and could articulate what they thought they wanted, even if it would likely change. The same was true when I interviewed M.B.A. candidates for Kellogg as a member of the admissions committee.

Many years later, as an executive recruiter interviewing senior executives, the same rules and approaches to interviewing still applied. The best candidates demonstrated self-awareness, focus, and clarity of expression. Regardless of where you are in your career, master the basics and you will nail every interview.

| Swab the Decks

In my years as an executive recruiter, real estate executive, mother, and friend, I've observed that making a great impression depends upon more than just what you wear and how you act. Ultimately it is how you feel about yourself that determines how you are perceived. Your energy precedes you and is palpable. Wear your confidence with ease.

In order for self-confidence to become as habitual as putting on your pants or brushing your teeth in the morning, you will need to be mindful of it. Whether you are age 15 and interviewing for your first job as a bagger at the supermarket (like I did when I was in high school), or you are mid-career and interviewing for the most important job of your life, you must follow a few basic rules and honor a few common courtesies in order to make a good impression. Here's a list of Do's and Don'ts for interviewing:

- **Do wear clothes that you have tried on in the last week and know are clean, pressed, and fit well.** Sit down in front of a mirror and look at yourself with a critical eye. Don't just look at yourself standing up. The interviewer will mainly see you while you are seated across the desk. This is no time to make a major fashion statement—unless you're interviewing at Vogue.
- **Do make a pit stop before going in; do a mirror check for lettuce in your teeth, lunch stains, and out-of-place hair or makeup.** Do a breath check. Use a mint, but do not go into an interview with gum in your mouth. I know this sounds like basic advice, but you'd be surprised how many people I've met with who could have used a gentle reminder.
- **Do be on time.** Allow time for traffic jams, for bad directions, and to get through building security. Call if you are going to be held up more than five minutes. If you arrive more than 10-15 minutes early, wait in a nearby coffee shop or outer lobby.
- **Do know the name, spelling, pronunciation, and title of the person or people you are meeting with when you introduce yourself to the receptionist.**
- **Don't harass the executive assistant—and don't flirt with him or her either.** The assistants are watching your every move and reporting back.
- **Do turn your cell phone off once you arrive at the interview, unless there is a chance you might hear from the interviewer.** Never answer a call or read a text during an interview; to do so is simply unforgivable, even if the interviewer doesn't honor the rule.
- **Don't use words and phrases that signal immaturity and a lack of professionalism.** Record yourself if necessary, and eliminate filler words that undercut your confidence, such as:
  "Stuff like that."
  "Like," and "You know."
  "Awesome."
  "You guys."

It's also important to remember that the same general rules that apply to most social situations apply to interviews as well: Avoid politics and religion, and don't complain about anything—the weather, directions, the coffee, anything! Keep the conversation upbeat and optimistic.

| Ready for Takeoff

You wouldn't go on a trip to Antarctica without knowing the facts, and you shouldn't go into an interview room without equipping yourself with the proper tools for survival. Just as it can get mighty cold at 50 below zero without insulated boots, your interview can turn chilly if you haven't packed enough background knowledge about the company, the position, and the interviewer.

I have found that job candidates can undermine strong communication and presentation skills by not having their facts straight or, worse yet, by failing to have done any homework at all.

- Consult the company website, annual report, Hoover's, and other resources to learn about the company, its history, lines of business, recent revenues, and stock price.
- Look for recent articles involving new launches, litigation, or senior leadership changes.
- Insist that you get a written position specification before you agree to an interview.
- Know as much as possible about the open position, the company, and your fit with the role and the organization. Write out a cheat sheet for yourself.
- Check in with your network to learn more about the position: Who was in it previously? Why is it open?
- Prepare 4-5 questions based on what you have learned; the questions should be relevant to the position you are seeking.
- Ask for or find a bio or résumé of the person with whom you are interviewing. If not on the company website (employer's or recruiter's), look on LinkedIn or Google the person's name.

| Managing the Interview

While you are by no means the captain of this ship, you are not at the mercy of the interviewer in an interview. You don't have to be pushy, but you must have an agenda, albeit secondary to that of the interviewer. Your primary goal is to convey key points about why you are qualified for this role, and you must deliver the same key points to everyone you meet (formally or informally) at that company.

Your secondary goal is to learn what you need to know to make an informed decision about the role if you get it. Going into the interview with a sense of confidence, composure, and a base of knowledge ensures that you will put your best foot forward. Here are a few more tips to make sure you dazzle your interviewer:

- It is imperative that you know how much time you have, so ask again, even if it was stated when the interview was scheduled; things change.
- Always go in with your 3–4 key talking points or affirmations. If you haven't made the points already, make sure you express them in a 2–3 minute summary statement before the interview is over.
- When you are asked more pointed questions, give examples and tell short stories about how you accomplished something; quantify as much as possible. For example:

  "The way we cut expenses was to analyze the distribution costs among the five regions. We saved 35% in the first year. My role was to provide a template to the five regional heads for an accurate comparison."

- Watch body language and other cues that you are holding the person's interest. If the interviewer looks bored, change your intonation or tap a pen. Also consider changing topics to get her or his attention.
- If you find yourself getting nervous or anxious, it is okay to pause and take a deep breath or ask for some water. Thinking carefully about your response to a question is perfectly acceptable, and is even preferable to giving an incomplete, rambling, or incoherent answer. (Tip: If you know you tend to get nervous, go to the washroom before the interview and put the insides of your wrists under cold running water. This literally cools your blood and will help to relieve anxiety.)
- If the interviewer is wasting time with idle chatter, get moving with something like *"I want to be respectful of your time, and I have some questions about the role, as well as a few points I want to leave with you about my background."*
- As a rule, don't bring up compensation. Ideally you know before the interview what the range of pay might be, so if you are

asked what you would want to be paid, you have a ballpark idea of how to respond.

- **If you run out of time, ask if you can send your questions via email.** It is a great way to thank the person formally and remain top-of-mind. Be sure the questions are uniquely relevant to that person.

| The Three-Minute Rule

As in sports, there are some basic rules of engagement and conduct for interviews. One of the most basic rules is that the response to a question is never simply yes or no. The interviewer is almost always looking for more detail, unless it's something like, "Are you a U.S. citizen?" Even then, start with yes or no and follow with a concise response, even if it repeats the elements of the question: "Yes, I am a U.S. citizen, though I was born in Canada."

Another basic rule is that no response should be longer than three minutes. I can't tell you how many interviews I have conducted in which people drone on for 10 minutes in response to a simple question. After three minutes, pause and ask interviewers if this is what they wanted to know before you go on.

Practice responding to common questions with friends using a timer. Then ask them to rate your response based on adherence to the rule, as well as the quality of the content. If it raises too many other questions, you are not packing enough relevant information into your three-minute response. Keep practicing—you'll get it!

| Going Against the Flow

Interviews shouldn't feel like interrogations; there should be an aspect of exchange during which you are able to assess the opportunity as well as convey your expertise and interest.

Many interviews turn into conversations, and in these cases your ability to go "off-script" is being evaluated. Listen and respond, but don't ask too many questions. The well-placed question shows you are interested, but a steady barrage can feel like an assault or a diversionary tactic.

The following are six common types of jobseekers/interviewees who go against the flow. Make sure you are not one of these! If you have experienced any of the warning signs, you may need to do more practice interviews with friends and supportive colleagues.

BLOWHARD This person is overbearing, boorish, egotistical, and can't wait to tell the interviewer all that he/she has done. This type has a tendency to oversell and to talk in terms of "I" rather than "we." The turnoff for the interviewer usually comes immediately.

Warning Sign: If the interviewer gets quiet and your time is cut short, you might be one of these types.

CHAMELEON This candidate is willing to be whomever the interviewer needs him or her to be—the classic "Jack/Jill of all trades, but master of none." The chameleon hasn't claimed a distinct skill set and therefore has no credibility, despite perhaps having strong interpersonal skills.

Warning Sign: If you feel like you have wandered off-track and lost yourself, you probably have failed to present your strengths. Reset your compass; there might still be time.

GAME PLAYER AND SIDELINER The game player has an ulterior motive largely unrelated to landing the available position. He or she might be feigning interest to force a promotion and/or a raise with a current employer. The sideliner is often a person who is a sought-after expert in a certain function and who interviews merely to feed his or her ego. The problem with these two types of interviewees is that their true motives might not be exposed for some time.

Warning Sign: When found out, word spreads quickly, and reputations can be permanently damaged. The risk is often not worth the reward, so don't play games or use an employer's or recruiter's time for selfish motives like feeding your ego.

RAMBLER This person doesn't know when to stop talking. Ramblers don't heed the three-minute rule when responding to a question. They are usually painfully unaware, and they might talk more and faster because they are nervous—a deadly combination.

Warning Sign: Pay attention to cues from interviewers. Are they tapping their pens, looking at their watches, or looking just plain uninterested? Stop talking!

SERIAL SHOPPER This interviewee type is enamored by choices. They will regularly interview with a variety of recruiters and prospective employers just to "see what's out there" and/or to compare opportunities with a current job. Sometimes the pattern shows up in job-hopping on the résumé.

> Warning Sign: This kind of "shopping around" is not part of a thoughtful strategy; you are being opportunistic and non-committal. You probably don't have a target, much less a bull's-eye.

| Employer Versus Recruiter Interviews

As part of my job as a recruiter, I interviewed candidates before their job interviews with employers. The biggest mistake people made was not being able to tell me specifically what they did at their previous job and how they did it. I am always looking for context, and anyone in a hiring position will be too. Once I know someone (a) is qualified from an experience perspective, and (b) possesses strong interpersonal and communication skills, then I want to know that the way the person works is compatible with the needs of my client, the employer.

When I asked a man who had a tremendously impressive résumé what he had done for seven years at a financial services company, he parroted his job description from his résumé. He could not tell me how exactly he achieved results. He did not quantify anything, provide any sense of his leadership style and approach, or even express his preferences for certain tasks and working environments. When I asked pointedly about what he did on the first day of his new assignment in Tokyo, he started his response with an oddly detached "What one would do..." At that point I put down my pen, a gesture meant to indicate the interview was going poorly, and a gesture which he didn't seem to notice. I concluded, in spite of his impeccable academic pedigree and distinguished military service, that he lacked self-awareness and was unable to demonstrate real problem solving or innovative thinking.

Lack of self-awareness can kill your chances in an interview. Your success in an interview is rooted in the knowledge of your personal geography. The people who impress me most can describe where they've been, where they are going, and why what they've done will move them from one place to another. The résumé is a piece of paper (or information on a computer screen) that serves as a ticket to get you through the door. The interview is a chance to demonstrate what you know and get yourself in the game.

Interviews are basically the same, whether in-house or with a recruiter. A recruiter can give you feedback to improve your interviewing skills and presentation for their client, but do not consider the recruiter interview less valuable or important. Recruiters can be key players in your network and overall strategy. Bring your best game.

| The Bad Interviewer

People often assume that the person interviewing them is experienced and/or skilled at interviewing. Remember that those who are experienced aren't always skilled, and vice versa. Then there are those interviewers who just have a bone to pick for no apparent reason. Some interviewers can be antagonistic, difficult, and downright rude. Here are some things you can do if you feel you are in this situation:

- Respectfully stop the interview by saying something like "It seems this conversation isn't progressing well, and we should think about either rescheduling or cancelling further interviews if I am not meeting your expectations."
- Immediately go to the human resources professional or executive recruiter working on the search to express concerns about the "productivity" of the discussion and your desire to be further considered on the condition that you get another interviewer. Most companies care about their reputations as employers and don't want them tarnished by bad apples. The recruiter, human resources person, or hiring manager should arrange another interview with someone of a similar level who can more respectfully represent them.
- In all cases you should remain poised, gracious, and professional. Don't let one bad apple spoil your chances for a great opportunity.

| Interview Follow-Up

The way you follow up after an interview might not always help your chances of winning the opportunity to reach your goal, but remember that bad form certainly can diminish your chances of getting anywhere. Here are a few guidelines to make sure there are no faux pas:

SENDING THANK-YOU NOTES In this age of electronic mail, I find thank-you emails acceptable, but handwritten notes remain more memorable. Even though the note takes a few days to arrive via "snail mail," it can often convey a personal touch that stands out. It only needs to be a few lines to leave a good impression (no flowery, scented stationary). And yes, send a personalized note to every person you interviewed with. Don't just copy everyone on one group email.

FOLLOW-UP MATERIALS If you talked to your interviewer about forwarding a list of references, a more detailed résumé, or a writing sample, send those pieces along electronically as soon as possible. It is even appropriate to attach them to your thank-you note. Similarly, the thank-you note is a good place to pose any remaining questions you might not have had time to ask during the interview.

CALLING FOR UPDATES A good recruiter/interviewer will have made an assessment and/or gotten feedback from other interviewers as soon as possible so that the impressions are fresh. Ideally they will take the initiative to follow up with you in a few days to keep the process moving. However, there are times when they need to interview other candidates over a period of a week or more to be able to compare and rank the candidates and determine next steps. Unless instructed otherwise, after one week it is appropriate to call or email the lead interviewer or recruiter to ask for feedback and get an update. Don't stalk. If you don't get a response, wait a few days. If you have other offers, convey that to your contact, but never misrepresent the other offers to try to elicit a response—it will surely come back to haunt you.

| Handling Rejection

No one likes rejection, but it is an inevitable part of life. Whether being turned down for a date, a mortgage, a college application, or a job you interviewed for, the initial sting is always the worst. You just can't take it personally. I know, this sounds trite, but it's so true: It is important not to take it personally. No one is saying you are a bad person; they merely mean that you are not right for the position relative to others who were in play. Come to grips with what might have gone wrong, and praise yourself for what you did right. Follow these tips to move on with your dignity intact:

DON'T PUT ALL YOUR EGGS IN ONE BASKET Even if you believe you were born for this job, you aced the interview, and there could be no better person for it, you don't know the politics, the qualifications of other candidates, or other factors that could have made them go with someone else. Always pursue multiple opportunities simultaneously so you aren't devastated at having to start over from the beginning.

GET FEEDBACK Respectfully probe interviewers to find out what aspect of your background or style fell short. Sometimes you find that what is on the job specification isn't really what they want now that they've seen several live bodies. Don't force the issue; sometimes they can't put their finger on what it was and can only say that they liked someone else better.

DON'T ARGUE Don't shoot yourself in the foot by debating the decision. I once had a candidate take issue with my assessment of his qualifications relative to the job specification. I had to let him know that his attitude was putting him at risk of not being considered for anything by the firm—ever—if he persisted. Arguing persistently in this situation is a death knell that announces the end of the professional relationship.

BE GRACIOUS The way you handle the "turnoffs" (as recruiters call them) says much to interviewers about your character and whether they might consider you for something else. After receiving feedback, thank the person for their time, and ask to be considered for other openings and to be kept in mind if the preferred candidate doesn't work out (it happens). Send appropriate thank-you notes.

Entry Level

Your interview comments should convey ambition and knowledge of the role. In the interview, use coursework and projects from your studies, as well as in-service training from summer jobs or internships, as substitutes for years of experience.

Mid-Level

Raise your hand for every relevant internal opportunity—if only to build your interview skills. Express your developing expertise. Be explicit about the kind of new role you seek and which skills are transferable, and acknowledge gaps.

Executive Level

You should be getting pretty good at this by now. Even if you have been with the same company a long time, at this point you should have sought at least a few opportunities for internal interviews like the ones mentioned above. If you are rusty, consider going to a seminar sponsored by your alma mater's career or placement office to brush up on interviewing techniques.

Encore Level

In the interview discussion, bring your passion, energy, and wisdom to bear. Whether you are staying in the for-profit workforce or volunteering at a not-for-profit, make no excuses for your age. Position it as an advantage and a chance for the employer to inject maturity, stability, and leadership into an important role.

Detour Route

It is critical that you weave a cohesive story of your past and current situation. Never lower your head in shame about anything you have done; anticipate questions by offering your rationale for past moves and what you learned from them. Similarly, state in no uncertain terms your case for where you see yourself going—role, title, compensation. Arrive having thought these things through, and know your value.

ARRIVING AT YOUR DESTINATION

"MANY OF LIFE'S FAILURES ARE PEOPLE WHO DID NOT REALIZE HOW CLOSE THEY WERE TO SUCCESS WHEN THEY GAVE UP."
- THOMAS EDISON

10

NEGOTIATING AN OFFER AND THE FIRST 100 DAYS

"Achievement of your happiness is the only moral purpose of your life, and that happiness, not pain or mindless self-indulgence, is the proof of your moral integrity, since it is the proof and the result of your loyalty to the achievement of your values." ~ Ayn Rand

Although the world of work continues to change constantly, the rules of negotiation remain largely unchanged. With so many companies seeking ways to cut costs and get more productivity out of fewer employees, you might think you have little room to maneuver; however, in an effort to manage retention costs (which are more substantial per employee than you might think), many companies negotiate up front to ensure that the employees they *do* hire are working at an optimum level. Smart employers recognize that many people are dealing with complex family situations and go to greater lengths to make sure that employees have what they need to achieve a fulfilling work-life balance.

We've shifted away from the traditional corporate ladder model, and many people now follow a nontraditional career path. In the new world of work, the career track looks more like latticework than like a ladder. Deloitte Touche Tohmatsu Limited have created the Mass Career Customization model, which involves a corporate career lattice for each employee. (Cathleen Benko and Anne Weisberg, both of Deloitte, are authors of *Mass Career Customization: Aligning the Workplace with Today's Nontraditional Workforces*, Harvard Business School Press, 2007.) Workers are strategically re-deployed depending on which jobs need to be done. Flexibility ranks high on the list of must-haves for many employees, and employers are increasingly willing to offer it. The personal situations of employees are much more likely to be taken into account today than they were even ten years ago.

| The Bottom Line

Before you ever think of entering a negotiation, you need to do your homework. By doing some research through helpful contacts and publicly available information (start with the company's online postings to calibrate), you can usually find out what the appropriate range of compensation is for a given position. A number of sites on the Internet list salary and bonus ranges for various positions.

You can look on job websites for comparable positions, and there are also compensation studies put out by reputable consulting firms. These studies provide greater detail, both current and historical, by industry, rank, function, and location. Some companies use these studies to calibrate their own salary ranges. Be advised that ranges may vary wildly, and be sure to use only current and relevant information from contacts within your network who are in proximity to the region in which you'd be working.

The general rule is never to discuss salary until the prospective employer asks about your expectations and earning history. Whether you found the job online or through a recruiter, you probably were given some idea of the range. When a job candidate learns the compensation and benefits being offered, these realities sometimes come as a surprise—and not always a pleasant one. With companies both large and small slashing benefits and perks, you need to prepare yourself mentally for this conversation.

When you are asked, be clear (and honest) about what you are currently making (or most recently made) and what your expectations and needs are. Do your best to make sure they are anchored in reality and in line with what the company currently offers employees—not with a model that no longer exists.

| Negotiating the Offer

When all is said and done and a job offer is on the table, you may think you have made it through the door and into a new position. Not quite. I have seen many job candidates blow opportunities at this stage. Those who have an offer withdrawn managed somehow to upset the delicate balance of wants, needs, and etiquette during sensitive negotiations.

The biggest mistakes I've seen occurred when candidates misrepresented the facts. One senior executive presented an inflated description of his compensation package, apparently forgetting that his previous employer was a Fortune 100 firm and that the details of his compensation package were public information. In another instance a company offered to purchase the house of a prospective executive to facilitate his relocation, and the candidate tried to include $200,000 worth of pricey upgrades in the purchase price. I advised the client that the original purchase price of the house was a matter of public record, and I suggested that my client consider withdrawing the offer because the candidate had shown such a lack of integrity. The candidate backpedaled furiously. In the end, my client was willing to forgive the transgression but only covered the executive's loss on the house.

Prospective employers are watching how you handle yourself in negotiations as an indicator of your character, judgment, and skill—regardless of the role you will play in their organization. If you have specific cultural or religious needs or have an unusual family situation, you need to bring those facts up. Timing is everything, and it is a mistake to wait until the final hour before an offer is tendered to mention your potential deal-breakers.

I recommend being completely transparent about lifestyle needs and requirements rather than risk uprooting your life for a situation where you or your family members will be miserable.

Similarly, you need to assess your prospective employer to make sure you are dealing with people who embody integrity and who value fairness. Trust matters on both sides as you establish a working relationship, but so does being true to yourself. This is business, so don't be naïve or gullible. There are times when you need to bend and times to hang tough, but listen to your intuition if you see warning signs early on. It's far better to walk away than to sign on with a company that causes you concern.

HERE ARE SOME RED FLAGS:

- The company fails to put the offer, including compensation, job description, and title, in writing.
- The company is quick to call attorneys into the negotiations.
- The person with whom you've been negotiating or to whom you thought you'd be reporting is no longer there.
- If you detect any evidence of certain "-isms"—e.g., nepotism, cronyism, favoritism, racism, sexism—at any point, even at this late stage of the game, run!
- Pending litigation for unfair employment practices.

| An Offer on the Table

Time is of the essence, so don't delay. Offers are perishable; they often won't last for more than a week. Do some homework, but be selective by seeking advice only from reliable sources. When the offer does appear, you want to have the information necessary to be decisive.

I once had a candidate who negotiated (through me) with my employer client for a week after receiving his offer. At the end of the week, he called to say he had just gotten a promotion with a pay raise at his current job. Coincidence? Hardly! This bum had been playing my client—and me—just to get his current employer to give him a promotion and a raise.

In hindsight, the way he threw petty issues into the negotiation should have tipped me off. He was stalling, waiting for the counteroffer from his employer. Counteroffers can arise, but more often than not, when you tell your current company you are resigning, that employer will let you go and take it as a sign your needs aren't being met—no harm, no foul. This willingness to part amicably makes this tactic not only a waste of time for the recruiter and the recruiter's client; it exposes the candidate to considerable risk as well.

If you are waiting for a specific offer and another one comes in first, do a quick gut check. If this offer was a "backup" job you simply don't want and wouldn't take under any circumstances (though let's hope you didn't always feel that way about it), respectfully decline the offer without negotiation. Do not, under any circumstances, take everyone through the process just to test your negotiating skills. You will likely be found out, and your reputation will be damaged; word spreads.

| Beyond Money

Before you overthink the salary component of the offer, put it in context. For example, if you are relocating, get a sense of the cost of living in the new city so youto know what to negotiate for. If you have been living in a major metropolitan area like Chicago, New York, San Francisco, or Los Angeles, the cost of living is considerably higher than it will be in Des Moines, Portland (Oregon or Maine), or Bentonville, Arkansas. You can calculate the difference on numerous websites, such as Homefair.com or Bestplaces.net. The employer extending the offer to you has likely factoredtaken the cost of living into consideration. Most companies base salary ranges for all employees in a certain location on local housing, grocery, and school costs, as well as taxation rates and so on.

Money, however, is not everything. Remuneration can take many forms. Here are some ways you can be compensated beyond a salary:

BONUS This can be paid in cash or in equity and often involves a stated formula (e.g., 30% of salary paid annually). Exemplary performance can earn you more, while substandard performance can earn you less. Recently the trend has been that the percentage of the bonus calculation determined by company performance has been increasing, while the percentage based on your individual performance has been shrinking.

SIGN-ON BONUS This bonus is paid out sometime between your acceptance of the position and your first day reporting to work. It is often paid to make up for a "loss" someone is taking on a portion of compensation at the job they are leaving. For example, if you are changing jobs in June, but the bonus at your old job isn't paid until January, your new employer might be willing to pay you up to 50% of your anticipated bonus as a sign-on bonus to cover the amount you would have earned had you stayed at your old job. Sign-on bonuses can be a way to keep you in a certain pay band instead of rolling the money into your salary or equity and causing inequities among your peers. Sign-on bonuses usually carry a stipulation that you have to stay in the job for a minimum period of time (typically a year) or you pay the bonus back to the company.

COMMISSION Some employers will offer a straight (100%) or partial commission scheme whereby you "eat what you kill." This is largely exclusive to sales-oriented roles in which you make your own destiny by generating fees or income through your efforts and earn a percentage of those fees for yourself. It is common in real estate leasing, insurance and securities brokerage, and retail. The good news is there is often no limit to what you can earn. The bad news: If you don't hustle, you don't eat. If commission-based compensation is common in your chosen function or industry, have an honest conversation with yourself about whether you (and your family) can stomach this arrangement. Some companies will offer an initial "draw" in which they will pay you what feels like a salary in the early months, but it is actually an advance against what you will eventually earn, so the pressure is still on to get out there and sell. If you are on straight commission, you might be entering into an independent contractor arrangement, versus that of an employee. The IRS cares about how you account for your income, and so does your employer. Be crystal clear on that point.

EQUITY At more senior levels, or if you bring a spectacular talent/skill set to the table, you can ask to earn stock or the right to buy stock at a set price. This can be a long-term wealth builder, assuming the company is doing well. Vesting is the speed with which you are assured 100% of those benefits when you leave the company. Accelerated vesting can be negotiated, meaning some people might work five years at one company before they are fully vested (at a rate of 20% per year), but you can ask for a three-year vesting (33.3% per year), giving you access to your money sooner (at least to borrow against).

PENSION OR RETIREMENT PLANS There are at least two types of common pension or retirement plans: "defined contribution" and "defined benefit." A defined contribution plan provides an individual account for each participant and for benefits based on the amount contributed to the participant's account, plus any income, expenses, gains, losses, and forfeitures of accounts of other participants that may be allocated to the participant's account. In a defined benefit plan, the amount (benefit) the employer will commit to paying you when you retire is based on a formula involving your age, wages, vesting (tenure), etc. In simpler terms, it is any plan that is not a defined contribution plan. This can be complicated, so take the time to review it with the company's compensation and benefits person and/or your financial planner or investment professional.

HEALTH BENEFITS In the U.S. these benefits are probably the most valuable to the employee and the most expensive for the employer. Although you don't select an employer based solely on their coverage, when all other things are equal, you should go with the one that provides better coverage for you and your family. The extent to which your employer offers domestic partner benefits, for example, can tell you how progressive they might be. There is little here to negotiate. The company will likely have a plan administered by an insurance company, and you are pretty much at the mercy of the coverage the employer has selected—unless you opt to pay more for supplemental insurance.

RELOCATION PACKAGE Many large companies will offer an allowance or cover expenses for you to move to your new location. It used to be a common practice for the company to buy your house and sell it, relieving you of the mortgage. Now, given how slowly homes sell, you will be lucky if the company pays for points on the sale of the old home and/or the purchase of a new home.

TEMPORARY HOUSING AND COMMUTING COSTS These can be part of a relocation package in which you are moving and need a place to call home every night, but you also have children who are finishing a school year and/or a trailing spouse who can't leave just yet. In this situation one might reasonably expect 3-6 months of housing costs (in a hotel or apartment); after that, this expense falls to you. The rationale is that the company wants you to move and become a permanent resident of the area, increasing the chances that you will stay in the job. In a similar scenario, an employer might pay for you to fly back and forth to your old home until the family has relocated. This compensation might be in the form of a monetary allowance or a certain number of flights per month for you or your spouse (children's travel is typically at your expense).

VEHICLE ALLOWANCE This perk is disappearing fast—except for the senior-most executives and those in sales who essentially work out of their cars. If you are lucky enough to get a vehicle allowance, the arrangement can be anything from dollars added to your paycheck that you apply to the cost of any vehicle you choose, to you being "given" a vehicle from a fleet the company leases, to you submitting your vehicle loan or lease payment and gas receipts for reimbursement. Be sure to ask about the tax treatment; you might have to pay taxes on the allowance as though it is regular income.

LUGGAGE ALLOWANCE Generally reserved for those executives who travel extensively, luggage allowances are becoming a relic of the past. Get one if you can!

CLUB MEMBERSHIP A scrumptious benefit if you can swing it. Again, this perk is usually reserved for the senior management and facilitates the lifestyle of the well-heeled executive who plays golf, works out at health clubs, and is a member of exclusive professional clubs. The idea is that your membership or participation in these clubs accrues to the benefit of the company by exposing you to people who can become clients or customers.

FINANCIAL OR TAX PLANNING ALLOWANCE The financial or tax planning allowance is generally for people whose finances are very complex because of their substantial earnings.

FLEXTIME, PARENTAL LEAVE, SABBATICAL These work-life related programs and provisions are increasingly important to employers as they can aid in the retention of good employees. Understand what these policies are before you start so there are no surprises when, for example, you decide to adopt a child or need time to care for an ailing parent.

TELECOMMUTING With companies' increasing consciousness of their employees' need for flexibility—as well as concern over their carbon footprints—some are giving employees the option of working from home a certain number of days per week. Recent studies have proven that employees who work from home are often more productive than those who come in to the workplace.

The benefits described above represent only an abbreviated overview of what companies might offer and what you might ask for in the way of compensation and benefits. Be sure before you ask for something that it is within the realm of possibility or you will look foolish.

| Negotiating on Your Own

Most negotiations should be straightforward enough for you to negotiate the terms of employment (or engagement in the case of an independent contractor) on your own. In fact, many jobs require no real payroll and benefits negotiation, just clarification and agreement. However, if you find you need more money or generally more favorable terms, don't turn into a ferocious warrior armed for big game. Stay positive, congenial, and open-minded.

- **Keep copious notes from earlier interviews and conversations.** Compare the actual offer to what might have been said. While the written offer is the binding one, sometimes the person who wrote it (someone in human resources, for instance) wasn't the person extending it (perhaps the hiring manager), and there has been an oversight or something has gotten lost in translation. Bring any sticking points to your contact's attention respectfully.

- **Pull out the research you have been gathering on compensation ranges for comparable jobs, first at the company, then within the industry, and even within the geographic region.** You might need this information to make a case for yourself.
- **If there are terms you don't understand, now is the time to ask questions of the employer and/or an employment attorney.** Similarly, if considering tax implications, check in with your tax accountant or financial planner.
- **Wait until you have reviewed all the terms, and assemble a complete list of issues before responding with a counteroffer.** Review it yourself first to decide which are the most important items and which you can live without. Make one counteroffer. Once the employer has responded, address *only* those issues that are on the table. Resist the urge to introduce any new ones, or you may start negotiating against yourself and thereby lose credibility.
- **Watch the clock.** As we discussed, offers have an expiration date. If negotiations are becoming protracted (maybe because of the employer's fumbling), ask for a written extension, and do your best to honor the next date.

| Negotiating with a Recruiter

If you identified your opportunity through a recruiter, it can be hugely advantageous to work through that recruiter on at least some of the negotiations. Here's why:

- **The recruiter usually knows what the employer's upper limits of compensation are and can advise you and filter your requests to avoid ill will in the negotiations.**
- **Your recruiter also knows what market compensation packages for your role look like at other companies and can advise the client on what they need to pay to get and keep you.**
- **Sometimes lawyers are called in to navigate complex employment contracts.** They can add a layer of angst to the process that a recruiter can diffuse to help keep negotiations on track.
- **Retained recruiters earn a fee based on your (the placement's) total first-year cash compensation (usually excluding sign-on bonus or equity).** Recruiters stand to make a little more if your compensation package goes up. Keep in mind, though,

that they also want repeat business from the employer, so they are indeed serving two masters.

In my experience, as you get into the finer points of the negotiation (e.g., start dates, prior vacation plans that fall after a start date, parking options, and administrative support), you should be talking to the employer directly while keeping your recruiter informed.

| Employment Terms

Some companies will ask you to sign an employment contract that includes a length of time after which both parties have the option to renew. It is most likely that you will be an employee "at will"; you can quit when you want or can be fired when the company chooses.

If you find that the terms of employment are getting complicated (benefits, bonus calculation, severance terms, etc.), consult a lawyer or even retain one to represent you during these negotiations. If need be, the employer has its own lawyers who can talk to yours. Don't be too quick to "lawyer up," however, because it can signal that you are needlessly litigious or overly cautious. For a simple contract or agreement, having a conversation with a lawyer and taking the advice back to your prospective employer should suffice. A couple of common clauses to make sure you understand (and about which you should consider consulting an attorney, since they can be deal-breakers) are as follows:

NON-COMPETE AND NON-DISCLOSURE (CONFIDENTIALITY) AGREEMENTS These are usually sought when valuable relationships, knowledge, or intellectual property could be at risk. A senior investment banker might be precluded from working for the competition for 1-3 years after leaving her current firm because some of her clients—and their fees—might follow her to the new firm. The same agreement might keep you from taking any employees with you if you leave the company to start your own venture. If you work in the research department of a pharmaceutical company, where patents are invaluable, the firm might ask you to sign a non-disclosure agreement preventing you from sharing certain confidential information about the company's operations and intellectual property.

SEVERANCE CLAUSE This is a clause that defines how you will be compensated when you leave the company. It assumes your departure would not be "for cause" (in which case you did something inappropriate that caused them to fire you). Most of the packages I've seen lately are offered when the company is laying people off, but they can also come into effect when an employee chooses to leave after a certain tenure of service to the company or after a change of control (acquisition, merger, divestiture, etc.). Very often these clauses are renegotiated at the time of separation depending on the circumstances of the separation, the health of the company, and the like.

| When to Walk Away

Despite the effort you have invested in interviewing and even negotiation, there might come a time when you need to "abandon ship," or walk away from the offer. I have seen situations in which an employer changes a previously discussed compensation scheme to unfavorable terms or changes the responsibilities of the role due to other company changes. Keep in mind that during the 3-6 months you have been in discussions and interviews with the company, there may have been corporate changes that affect your position, such as mergers, strategy changes, or layoffs. Surely you have been tracking these events in the news, but it may not be clear how your role will be affected and what kind of negotiating leverage you have—or don't have.

If you haven't liked how the negotiations have progressed, your uneasiness may be a sign of things to come. Putting aside any possible personal idiosyncrasies of the lead negotiator, maybe a closer look at policy issues and the corporate culture have convinced you that this is a place in which you just don't want to be. Trust your instincts on this one, and maybe use your network or LinkedIn to have a quick conversation with a former employee of the organization to test your suspicions.

I have seen people decline an offer because the person to whom they would have reported left the company or moved to another group or location. While a job shouldn't hinge on the presence of one person, if this boss or sponsor was the primary reason for leaving a job you already have, then that person's absence could be a valid reason not to accept the offer. At a minimum, if you get the news during negotiations, the change is significant enough to merit your offer being extended until after you have met the replacement boss.

| When the Offer Goes Away

I've seen offers disappear under many different circumstances. Sometimes the potential employee simply fails to honor the deadline, and the offer is withdrawn. But most often the employer discovers an untruth, indiscretion, or instance of plain bad judgment during the negotiation.

During the reference and background check of a senior-level human resources executive who was a candidate in the final round of interviews for the most senior human resources role at a Fortune 100 company, a felony popped up. When confronted with this information, he admitted that he had taken the fall for a sibling who had committed a crime. Because he was a human resources professional who knew a lot about hiring practices, he was foolish to think his transgression wouldn't be discovered. In this case, even if he had come clean about everything during the interview, I still don't think he could have saved himself.

The fine print of most offers states that the offer is contingent upon the completion of such things as a physical, a psychological test, a drug test, and perhaps further reference checks. Many employers are now checking credit reports and legal backgrounds. Take these conditions of sealing the deal seriously.

Another candidate's background check showed that she'd sued two previous employers for discrimination and had more unsettled lawsuits pending. Once again, the offer was yanked off the table.

Be aware of new social media traps. One new hire found her job offer withdrawn within a few hours of tweeting about accepting "a lame job just until something better comes along." Her new employers let her know she'd been canned via a Twitter post of their own.

Reject the temptation to discuss job prospects openly on social networking sites like Facebook and Twitter until the contract is signed. Even then, continue to use good sense when revealing details that may be available to your prospective employer and new colleagues. Always be complimentary toward your "new home." Of course, be careful not to insult your former employer either.

Follow my advice and you'll experience nothing but smooth sailing into your new home port.

Entry Level

You have the least leverage in negotiations, but you can demonstrate your commitment to moving up by asking what you would need to do in the next 1-2 years to be promoted. Don't expect a written commitment, but work toward that goal and keep asking the question.

Mid-Level

Managing compensation expectations can be a challenge at this level. You might feel you have earned the right to a hike in salary to go along with broader responsibilities. If the powers that be just can't up the salary ante, consider asking for a written agreement for a certain percentage increase (within your stated range) at the end of a specific time period and on the condition that you have exceeded performance expectations. This lets them know you are confident in your capabilities and serious about moving up, even if they aren't willing to put it in writing.

Executive Level

A formal on-boarding plan at the executive level might feel remedial or unnecessary, but accepting the offer of extra attention and possible access can only help you. Part of the benefit of such structured programs is the mechanism for feedback. The feedback can work both ways, you receiving it as the "newbie" and your new employer who stands to gain a competitive advantage.

...continued on next page

...continued from previous page

Encore Level

Sometimes you bring with you old habits that trigger unnecessary reactions to simple questions. Leave old baggage at the door! One seasoned executive felt very anxious not knowing certain things in the early days of her first job in a different industry. Her boss let her know it was okay not to know—yet. Allow yourself time to get up the learning curve, but hurry up!

Detour Route

There is a possibility that you are not exactly what they were looking for—talented, valued, but not what they had an open requisition or job specification for. The company might well be creating a job for you, and even though the compensation is not quite where you were, the upside is that you are probably with a company that believes in you, and there is room to grow. In this situation you will be hard-pressed to make a strong case for better compensation, at least until you have proven your value. You might believe you offer more than they asked for in terms of experience, level, and reputation. What matters most is what the company believes your value to be relative to other employees. Their sentiments will likely be reflected in the package you are offered.

11

→ ## SAFE LANDING

"Dream no little dreams, for they have no power to move men's souls." ~ Johann Wolfgang von Goethe

What a journey it has been, but it isn't over. There are so many things you will have to contend with even in the excellent work circumstances that you have created. The goal is to continue to grow, anticipate, question, and enjoy. You have what you need to move successfully in whatever direction you choose. Here are a few parting thoughts I want to arm you with as I send you off into the new world of work. Bon voyage!

| Abandoning Ship: When to Leave Your Job

I've had blog followers say they "hate" their jobs. I hate to think that things have gotten so bad that you are in "hate" mode. Being unhappy, dismayed, and apathetic are all bad enough, but "hate?" Such a situation calls for immediate action.

Let's put together two plans. One plan entails coping and staying put until you can make a move. The other plan: Get out! The problem is that when you are in hate mode, it can be mentally and emotionally debilitating and depressing, so you must find diversions, both inside and outside of the workplace, to provide some momentary relief from the pain of hating what you are doing.

- **Get your head right** – Consciously shift your attitude, and refrain from announcing to anyone who will listen that you hate or even dislike your job.

- Find some positive people in your workplace who can talk you out of walking the plank and who can lift you up a little every day.
- **Figure out what makes your work so intolerable.** What can you do to stay with the employer but shift into a different role (e.g., take a class or get a degree)?
- **If a person you are working with or for is the bane of your existence, have you tried to reconcile possible differences, to make amends?**
- **If someone is legitimately abusive, find an ombudsman or other professional advocate with whom you can share this information.**
- **Have fun outside of work, but don't bring it to the workplace.** Continue to show up on time and in good form (not hungover, etc.); after all, you need good references.

If you have determined that your circumstances are unbearable and you run the risk of jeopardizing your self-esteem, or worse yet, "going postal," make a plan to get out.

- **Use the career map process to set about creating your job-hunting strategy.** It will probably take longer since you have a job, but be systematic and determined.
- **Don't broadcast that you are looking. Use days off to interview if you can.**
- **Try to limit your job-hunting efforts (online and via phone) to when you are at home or at least on your lunch break.** Your work email is never private, so set up a free email account with Google, Yahoo, or Hotmail for job-search purposes. If you use your work email address, potential employers will note your lack of discretion, not to mention the fact that you are using your current employer's resources inappropriately.
- **Give at least two weeks' notice before leaving any job so you aren't leaving anyone hanging or burning any bridges.** Put your resignation in writing and date it so your employer cannot claim that you left without giving reasonable notice.

| How to Leave Your Job

Whether you choose to leave after a stellar run with your employer or you are unceremoniously fired and escorted from the premises immediately, it pays to leave with dignity. The specific behaviors to avoid vary depending on the circumstance, but, above all else, when parting company you should always maintain your professionalism. Regardless of the circumstances of your leaving, here are some tips:

- If you have time before leaving, take personal items from your office or workspace, as well as documents you might have produced that can be useful to you but are not proprietary or confidential. (Be careful that anything you take would not be seen as proprietary or confidential from the company's standpoint, not just your own. Proceed with caution here.)
- Don't display greed and vindictiveness by raiding the supply closet and taking items that are not yours.
- Say goodbye to as many co-workers as possible, and exchange contact information.
- Ask to leave an outgoing voicemail message for a week or two after your departure that tells people calling in how to reach you.

If you have gotten a "pink slip," honor these basics:
- **If you are emotional, compose yourself.** Ask a friend to sit with you for a bit, but no crying, screaming, or storming out for general viewing.
- **Ask for an explanation if one is not given.** Don't argue; accept it. If you believe this is a wrongful termination, take it up with a lawyer after you've departed.
- **If your termination was not for cause, ask about severance in the form of cash and/or COBRA benefits; it always pays to ask.**
- **Do not bad-mouth people or the company on the way out, no matter how hurt or angry you might be.**

If you have the good fortune to be leaving of your own volition, don't get too giddy and forget to respect those you are leaving behind.

- As a show of respect, tell your superior/supervisor about your intention to leave first; tell others later.
- Give two weeks' notice if possible, recognizing that the company might ask you to leave earlier to minimize disruption or access to proprietary information in the event you are going to a competitor.
- Leave a status report on outstanding projects so that your successor can follow up on your work.
- **Offer to conduct an exit interview with your superior or human resources person.** This is where you can offer constructive feedback about what you enjoyed about your time there and what they might improve upon.

- **Ask those you worked with closely and hold in high regard if they are willing to be references for you if/when the time comes.** Offer to do the same for them.

| Starting Your Own Business

Tough times often fuel entrepreneurial ventures. In fact, some of the biggest business successes—Hyatt Corporation, Hewlett-Packard, Trader Joe's, CNN, and MTV, to name a few—were launched during economic downturns. The 2009 Kauffman Index of Entrepreneurial Activity shows that entrepreneurial activity rose from .32% in 2008 to .34% in 2009. That means 340 out of every 100,000 Americans started a business every month, the highest level since Kauffman started keeping tack in 1996.

Before you run out to hang your shingle, think about the reasons why you are doing it. Is it a knee-jerk reaction to being laid off, the realization of a lifelong plan, or something else? Whatever your rationale, test out the idea with the most trusted members of your network. Fill out your career map with this business as one of your verticals or industries. You must articulate the unique skills you are bringing to it, determine the gaps, target your clients or customers (instead of targeting companies), and choose your business partners and management team (your contacts, complete with action steps).

Consulting is a business many people choose as a permanent career move or as a stopgap while they are looking for work or waiting for economic conditions to change. In *The Consultant's Calling*, Geoffrey M. Bellman writes, "Consulting work is about succeeding as yourself, being yourself more often than playing a role." There is no getting around this self-knowledge stuff. As a consultant you will define your success differently and will probably deploy your skills in different ways, sometimes in ways you might not have anticipated.

Even though I was considered a consultant while working as an executive recruiter, the consulting work I offer corporate clients through my company, Talent Optimization Partners, LLC, is not search; I offer talent management and recruitment consulting. After forming the business, I spent a couple of months testing my services pitch on some friendly former clients to get feedback on the services and the marketing materials. The feedback was good enough to encourage me to keep pushing and making refinements.

The real "aha moment" didn't come until I sat with prospective clients who asked me to consult on issues related to diversity recruiting. This arena is something that I know how to do exceptionally well (you might recall that I co-founded Spencer Stuart's diversity practice and led it for 10 years), but I hadn't included it in my offerings! I was so intent on offering things I *thought* people wanted that I neglected a treasure trove of skills I can legitimately ask my clients to pay for.

Because entrepreneurship is not for everyone, here are a few things you need to think about as you contemplate starting your business:

- **Have more than a concept; write out a business plan, and make sure it includes a realistic timeline and budget.** The Small Business Administration has a business plan template you can download at *http://web.sba.gov/busplantemplate/ BizPlanStart.cfm*
- **Know your capital needs.** Consulting can require a laptop, phone, and printer, while a dairy farm requires land, cows, and a milking and distribution system, all of which will require financing.
- **Think through your human capital needs; leverage your network to build your team based on the gaps or roles you need filled.** You will probably want to partner with other contractors and consultants who offer complementary services so you can refer clients to them and receive referrals from them.
- **Allow yourself time to adjust to not going into the office like you used to, to traveling and dining out for business on your own dime, and to not having technological support.** Don't underestimate the shift you will be making as you disconnect your identity from your old job and link it to a new one of your own making.

| Overcoming Roadblocks

The following are some common roadblocks you may encounter in your journey and some proven measures for removing or otherwise dealing with them.

YOU'VE BEEN FIRED

Job loss ranks among the top 10 most stressful events in one's life. Job hunting doesn't make the top 10 list, but it is certainly one of the most anxiety-producing activities known to man. Letters and phone calls go unreturned. Family members who might have good intentions can pile on extra angst by constantly asking how things are going. You feel you are making absolutely no progress. It's easy to feel overwhelmed, panicked, irritable, and depressed, especially if finding a new job is taking longer than anticipated and financial pressures are mounting. There are a few things you can do to push through the tough times:

- **Breathe—really.** We hyperventilate when we are anxious, and this inhibits clear thinking. Calm down. Consider meditation; it got me through my divorce, and I still practice it.
- **Don't beat yourself up.** Forgive yourself for not having sent 10 letters last week; instead, praise yourself for sending four letters and for having three unplanned but productive phone calls, which resulted in two leads.
- **Chop your long to-do list down to just a few high-priority daily activities.**
- **Don't take rejection personally.** Reaffirm how wonderful you are, and put yourself near other people who can validate your wonderfulness!
- **If you keep running into roadblocks, you are likely on the wrong road. Reassess and reroute.**
- **Don't take all the advice that is given.** Stay focused on your strategy and goals, and be discerning even with well-wishers.
- **If you are drinking alcohol, taking medication more than usual, having trouble sleeping, or finding it hard just to get out of bed, consult a physician or psychologist.** There is no shame in asking for help.
- **Envision yourself healthy, prosperous, and successful.** If you can't see it, it won't be possible.

OFFICE ROMANCE

Not only do most companies frown on office romances, your involvement with someone in your professional circle can put you and your reputation at risk—whether you are a man or a woman, married or single, gay or straight.

Make no mistake: Love happens. A dear friend of mine was approached at a conference by one of her top rivals from a competing firm who had taken a personal interest in her. She resisted his initial (and respectful) advances, but they were both single and had undeniable chemistry. A romance blossomed, and they kept their relationship under wraps for the first six months to see if it would last. It did; they competed against one another for business, and both continued to prosper at their respective companies.

The management was advised at both companies, and while a few competitive feathers were ruffled at my friend's firm, business results spoke for themselves and the romance was a nonissue. After nearly two years of dating and a relocation, they became engaged and were recently married—a very happy ending for two mature professionals who handled their relationship with aplomb.

However, many high-profile executives have crashed and burned because of clandestine office relationships or affairs; Harry Stonecipher at Boeing comes to mind. Boeing's board didn't take kindly to Mr. Stonecipher, a married man, having an affair with another Boeing employee, and he was forced to resign. Jack Welch, former CEO of General Electric, met Suzy Wetlaufer during an interview with *Harvard Business Review*. Ms. Wetlaufer served briefly as that magazine's editor in chief before she was forced to resign after admitting to having been involved in an affair with Welch while preparing an interview with him for the magazine. The couple married, have since authored several books together, and started a robust consulting business.

INAPPROPRIATE ADVANCES

I was a divorced, single mother for nearly half of my professional career and have had to deal with being propositioned by men in business settings. Men are just as likely to garner similar attention and overtures from women, and homosexual advances sometimes occur amongst both sexes. Whether it is a client, colleague, vendor, or other professional contact, the advance needs to be nipped in the bud.

One male friend recently told me of a situation in which a female former client called and asked him to bid on a six-figure contract. He spent two days putting together the request for proposal. Then he got a call from her announcing that another vendor had been chosen for the job, part of which would be carried out in his town. The reason for her call? She wanted to ask if the winning vendor could use his subcontractors for the job.

When he told me more of the story, I learned that he had also put in a seven-figure bid a few years earlier at this same woman's behest—once again coming in first runner-up. Then came the kicker: While on a job where she was representing the client, she had propositioned him. He had turned her down.

The thing that was clear to me, but which my friend couldn't see, was that this woman was playing a passive-aggressive game. She wants an excuse to stay in touch with him, so she occasionally dangles a seemingly incredible opportunity in front of him even though she probably has no intention of ever letting him get a job from her employer again. My advice to him was to find a way to get in touch with the real decision-maker, her boss. I told him that he should maintain a cordial relationship, but that he shouldn't ever expect to land the contract as long as she's standing between him and her boss.

You can be subject to everything from the spurned would-be lover in the story above, to the seemingly inadvertent touch of a certain part of the body, to a creepy "compliment," to an outright, obnoxious, sexually explicit comment or joke. Here is my general (non-legal) advice when encountering those unwanted overtures:

- Remain calm, and don't overreact or call negative attention to yourself or the offender as it is happening.
- Consider looking the person in the eye and telling him or her you did not appreciate the advance or comment and that you hope it never happens again.

- **In some cases what is perceived as inappropriate was inadvertent, unintended, misconstrued, or just stupid.** Forgive, but don't forget.
- **Don't tempt fate.** Watch your wardrobe and behavior in work settings. Flirtation and innuendo can send mixed messages.
- **Be aware that certain settings can increase the likelihood of these occurrences, and buddy up or have a plan of exit if things are heating up.** I am talking about work settings that take on a social air—after hours, retreats, conferences, etc.
- **Drinking can drastically lower people's inhibitions.** Watch your consumption so you always have your wits about you and can fend off unsavory elements.
- **Don't be a victim. Stand up for yourself, but know when to ask for help, whether physical or legal.**
- **Depending on the severity of the transgression, consider the consequences of making an issue of it.** Try the direct approach first. You don't want to get into "your word against his/hers."
- **Being more junior in rank can make it tough to push back.** If there is a pattern of bad behavior, advise a trusted higher-up and consider legal remedies if push comes to shove.

| It's a Small World: A Diversity Discussion

The following are some observations and opinions that are derived from the ten years that I co-founded and led Spencer Stuart's global Diversity Practice.

WHAT IS DIVERSITY?

The term "diversity" is defined in the U.S. as "people of color," women, or underrepresented groups—LGBTQ, people with disabilities, etc. It is generally born of a post-segregation society and is the most recent and palatable incarnation of affirmative action. Many corporations have added the term "inclusion" to include individual characteristics beyond those people are born with (gender, ethnicity, etc.), bringing in those that are learned and/or chosen (values, religion, language education, income, interests, etc.).

The benefits of investing in diversity and inclusion are many, but the most important is that a diverse and inclusive workforce drives diversity of thought and innovation. Companies can't foster innovation if they keep the same people they have always had at the table.

The best-performing companies hire the best people—from all over the world! The global economy dictates that all companies adopt a paradigm shift to attract and retain the best talent—regardless of gender, race, ethnicity—in order merely to survive, let alone thrive.

WHAT DOES THIS MEAN TO YOU?

- You will do well to select employers who demonstrate a commitment to diversity and inclusion as a basic talent management tenet.
- Assist your employer in understanding diversity and inclusion beyond the traditional metrics or quotas.
- Expose yourself to global opportunities—those companies that will value your skills and talents—wherever they are in the world.

| Women in the Workforce

The biggest challenge women face in the workforce is finding or helping to create a level playing field. No one is looking for a handout, just a meritocracy and a culture that values difference, no matter what it looks like, sounds like, or where it is from. Women need to take a more aggressive stance in advocating for ourselves; that is, we need to tell employers what we need to be productive in the workplace.

Some employee resource and affinity groups are already doing this work, but whether individually or as a group, we need to manage our careers actively and do as my father told me: "Tell people what you want!" Women have a legacy of managing multiple dimensions of life—children, home, parents, etc.—so that is not new and won't change. Luckily, I think men are starting to face similar challenges and are gaining an appreciation for the work-life balance that used to be a women's issue only.

There is a growing contingent of women who don't simply want the "prize" of reaching the highest levels of an organization anymore. There is a price that both men and women pay to attain the loftiest of corporate heights, but women often make even bigger sacrifices when it comes to childbearing, child-rearing, and other familial obligations. Those considerations, coupled with the stress of needing generally to be "twice as good to get half as far," can be quite discouraging and leave some women saying it is not worth it.

Add to that the pay disparity between men and women (women make about 77 cents on the dollar compared with men) and it's easy to understand why women are increasingly starting small businesses with the hope of leveraging their skills on a more level playing field. According to the U.S. Small Business Administration, between 1997 and 2004 the growth in the number of businesses owned by women (at least 51% of owners are women) was nearly 2 1/2 times the rate of all U.S. privately held firms (22.9% versus 9%). Furthermore, employment in these firms grew more than three times faster than in all other firms (39% versus 11.6%), according to estimates from the Center for Women's Business Research. These statistics are encouraging, to say the least. Let's go, girls!

| Workplace Paradigm Shift

I think corporate America is still stuck under the old assimilation paradigm, in which men have set the norm. A lot of the negative stereotypes about women's and other underrepresented groups' intellect, drive, commitment, intestinal fortitude, leadership abilities, risk tolerance, etc. still exist among many of the leaders making hiring and promotion decisions. Further, many leaders simply have never been trained or expected to make competency-based decisions; instead they have hired people with whom they are the most comfortable and whom they see succeeding in the organization. In other words, they hire those in their own image.

Few of these leaders are held accountable for making thoughtful assessments. Sometimes a small part of their compensation might be tied to diversity metrics, but rarely is it substantial enough to change behavior or alter a culture. What's the answer? Read on.

12

ALL ABOARD: CORPORATE, NOT-FOR-PROFIT, AND ADVISORY BOARDS

"Whatever you do or dream you can do—begin it. Boldness has genius and power and magic to it." ~ Johann Wolfgang von Goethe

For many executives, being a member of a corporate, not-for-profit (NFP, a.k.a. "nonprofit organization" or NPO), or advisory board is a clear objective that will advance their career opportunities through skill building, visibility, and access. For others it is a structured way to be of service to a not-for-profit or a for-profit enterprise by sharing their unique skills and insights. For still others, it is a badge of honor worn proudly to suggest they have "arrived" and have been admitted to an elite, exclusive club with special privileges bestowed upon them (including income).

These reasons and objectives for board service are not mutually exclusive, and most are respectable. Some people have purely selfish agendas and motives, such as increasing their retirement income stream or gaining access to influential businesspeople who can help grow their business (at least ostensibly). Nevertheless, there remains a mystique and sometimes naïveté about the characteristics boards are seeking in a director, member, or trustee and how you can position yourself for consideration. In this chapter we will look at an overview of the responsibilities of a board and its directors, demystify the recruitment and selection process, and discuss how board membership can be an important part of building skills to enhance your career.

Let me be clear about my exposure to and expertise with boards. As an executive recruiter I worked on numerous board searches for public companies (though I was not a formal member of the boards' practice) and had countless executives plead with me to divulge the secrets of board readiness and recruitment (which I will do here). I have also been a director of a publicly traded company, Medical Properties Trust (NYSE: MPW) since 2004, where I have served on the audit committee and now serve on the compensation committee and the nominating and governance committee.

Finally, I currently serve on the board of a not-for-profit organization. I held off joining a not-for-profit board for many years because as a single mother who traveled extensively, I knew I didn't have much control over my travel and would likely miss many of the board meetings; furthermore, I wanted to devote my downtime to my son. I may have missed out on valuable contacts that could have advanced my career faster, but it was a tradeoff I consciously accepted.

I joined the board of the Chicago Sinfonietta, "The World's Most Diverse Orchestra," when I knew I was leaving Spencer Stuart and would have more time to commit to fulfilling my responsibilities as a board member. I also wanted to direct more of my time to performance arts and demonstrate to my son (a budding thespian) that one has to support the arts beyond simply buying tickets. This is the context from which I will be drawing to discuss corporate and civic boards.

| Corporate Boards

The responsibilities of a corporate board director are many, and the stakes are high—these public companies fall under the scrutiny of state and federal regulatory agencies and legal jurisdictions. Directors are elected by the shareholders and have a fiduciary responsibility to those shareholders as the highest authority in the management of the organization. In other words, the CEO or highest-ranking employee of a publicly held entity is accountable to the board of directors. Attendance at board meetings is important, as is participation on at least one of the board committees. These committees typically include the following:

- Compensation
- Audit
- Finance
- Governance/nominating
- Ethics/social responsibility

A corporate board's range of oversight includes providing input on strategic plans and policies, compliance with regulatory requirements, and assessment of the performance of the company and its senior leaders. Directors have a duty of care to act in the best interest of the shareholders. They also have a duty of loyalty, which means they must be clear of any conflicts of interest with the company on whose board they sit. These conflicts can be of a personal nature (e.g., familial relations or personal financial holdings) or business interests (e.g., ownership of related entities or customer/vendor relationships).

Lastly, directors have a duty to avoid intermingling corporate and personal assets. Corporate directors can be subject to personal liability if they have been found to be negligent in honoring any of the duties mentioned above. For that reason, many boards purchase directors and officers liability insurance (D&O) to protect their directors against lawsuits.

Corporate directors have a fiduciary responsibility to shareholders and therefore are responsible for making sure the company's finances are in order. This includes paying attention to liquidity, capital reserves, approving a budget, and ensuring adherence to it. The audit committee, which is made up of inside directors (management team members of the company) and outside (or independent) directors, works closely with the company's chief financial officer and the outside auditors to review audited, independent financial statements.

| Sarbanes-Oxley

In 2002, on the heels of several corporate scandals that led to the failure of companies such as WorldCom, Enron, and Adelphia, President

George W. Bush signed into law a bill sponsored by U.S. Senator Paul Sarbanes (D-MD) and U.S. Representative Michael G. Oxley (R-OH). That legislation is commonly known as "Sarbanes-Oxley," "SOX," or the "Public Company Reform and Investor Act." Among other things, this act charges boards of directors, specifically audit committees, with overseeing financial reports on behalf of investors. This landmark legislation called for greater oversight, accountability, and independence for public company management teams and boards.

The recent economic recession, caused in part by the near collapse of our financial system, cast a light on corporate governance and accountability for all organizations and for financial services companies in particular. Fingers continue to be pointed and policies evaluated, but clearly shareholders are scrutinizing management and boards of directors more carefully than ever. Executive compensation is the number-one area of scrutiny and is widely believed to be excessive relative to corporate profits.

CEO succession is another burning issue for most corporate boards since, according to Spencer Stuart, "the median tenure as sitting CEO for the top 100 CEOs has remained at five years for the past two years" ("Route to the Top," 2008). Boards often outlast management teams and need to assess leadership talent against the evolving strategic needs of the company.

This brings me to the important and related issue of risk management. This discipline goes beyond insurance to include looking at events or situations that could either benefit or imperil an organization. It encompasses virtually all functions, including strategic planning, accounting, and operations; it is a frequent agenda item at board meetings.

| Board Readiness and Recruitment

Board seats, whether not-for-profit, corporate, or advisory, are typically reserved for executive-level professionals who have experience and expertise they can bring to bear on the company's strategic direction. Some would argue that corporate boards were historically exclusive men's clubs where current and retired CEOs could still contribute their expertise, catch up with old friends, and get paid a handsome stipend (plus stock) for their time.

More recently, sitting CEOs have been prevented by their own boards from sitting on more than 1-3 other public company boards because of the increased time and preparation required for outside boards, the need to focus on their own company performance, and possible liability (not to mention bad press). Sarbanes-Oxley required board members to be more independent, so there are fewer current employees (inside directors) serving, and the outside directors go through a more rigorous vetting process, often facilitated by an executive search firm.

There is truth to the earlier "men's club" reference in that the CEOs of the country's largest public companies were exclusively men until Katherine Graham of the Washington Post Company became the first woman CEO of a Fortune 500 company in1963. Though she didn't formally assume the title until 1979, she took over after her husband's death in 1963 and chaired the board from 1973 to 1991. Whether sitting or retired CEOs, men have had the lion's share of board seats.

In the past, recruitment often meant inviting acquaintances from one's own business and social circles. Over time, as the complexities of global competition and capital markets emerged, board recruitment became increasingly strategic. That is, boards began to be more deliberate about the industry and functional expertise required of their directors. Add the increased expectations of independence that Sarbanes-Oxley imposed, and you find that board recruitment has become a process taken very seriously by boards and shareholders alike.

According to the 2009 Spencer Stuart board index, "58% of director nominations came from executive search firms, 21% from non-management (outside) directors, 14% from company CEOs, and 6% from other insiders (e.g., controlling shareholders, other executive officers)." Given the proportion of director nominations coming from search firms, you certainly want to be known by the top firms (Korn Ferry, Heidrick & Struggles, Spencer Stuart, Russell Reynolds, and Egon Zehnder). However, consideration is very much dependent upon your reputation preceding you.

You can serve yourself up directly to the search firms, CEOs, and others mentioned in the statistics above for board consideration. Recruiters constantly gather information from numerous sources (annual reports, financial statements, articles, and other executives) to get the skinny on various executives who might be worthy of consideration. Usually these data are gathered before a call is placed to you to learn of your possible interest and/or availability. The recruiters already know what other public boards you are on and whether you are "overboarded" or coming off of one soon. They might already have called executives with whom you have worked to test your reputation and perceived expertise.

I know a considerable number of people in both my personal and professional spheres who have been offered board seats based on recommendations from people they have worked with at their day jobs or on not-for-profit boards. In my own case, I was asked to sit on the board of Medical Properties Trust (MPT) by the chief financial officer of the company. The CFO had been a CFO candidate of mine for a search client two years before he called me; he had turned down my client's offer to join MPT when it was a startup.

Medical Properties Trust is a real estate investment trust (REIT) that was about to file its initial public offering (IPO) when they asked me to consider the board. They were interested in me because of my past real estate experience, my search experience, and my exposure to boards and governance issues. I was flattered but had to think long and hard. Being on a corporate board had not been on my radar, and more importantly, it involves serious responsibilities, potential liabilities, and time commitment.

I agreed to serve for four reasons:
1. I thought the company had a sound business strategy based on my knowledge of the real estate industry.
2. I thought I could benefit from learning more about the health care side of their business.
3. I liked and respected the management team and other directors, and I thought I could add diversity of thought.

4. I thought it would assist me in better understanding some of the governance issues my board search clients faced. I also liked what I had seen of Birmingham, Alabama, where they are based, and Alabama was my mother's home state.

Here is what you must do if you want to be considered seriously for a public company board:

- **Google yourself. Know what publicly available information is out there.**
- **Know your reputation among the senior-most executives in your professional universe.** Ask a trusted colleague in order to get the truth.
- **Be able to articulate what makes you special and of value to a board.** Based on the preference for CEOs, division presidents, and other top management, if you are not at the right level, you will need functional, industry, and/or international expertise that is relevant to that company.
- **Be clear as to how the board seat will add to your career.** It is an honor to be asked, but beyond the flattery, it has to make sense.
- **Be honest about the resources—time and money—you can commit to this role.** Chronic absence from board meetings is taken seriously.

Also consider participating in one of the numerous seminars, "colleges," or webinars sponsored by business schools, executive search firms, and related magazines (e.g., Corporate Board Member and Directors & Boards). These sessions are always offered to current directors who are encouraged, if not mandated, by the board's governance committee to take courses every year or two in order to stay up to speed on legislation and topical issues of governance. Several of these courses are tailored to aspiring board candidates and might feature a résumé book or compilation of bios that goes to recruiters and nominating committees to increase the participant's chances of getting noticed and considered.

| Overview of Current Corporate Board Composition and Trends

Composition
- Only 16% of new directors are first-timers.
- Former CEOs, COOs, and the like account for 17% of new independent directors.

- **The average age of an S&P 500 board member is 61.7 years, versus 60.2 years in 1999.** The average age of newly appointed members is 56.5 years.

Desired Backgrounds
- **More than 70% of all new independent directors come from six fields:**
  - Consumer goods and services
  - High tech/telecommunications
  - Industrial/manufacturing
  - Financial services
  - Private equity/investments
  - Academia/not-for-profit
- **Nearly half of all corporate boards sought current top executives, while 34% looked for retired CEOs, COOs, etc.**
- **The actual number of newly recruited minority and women directors fell short of expressed demand.**
  - 50% said they wanted minorities, but only 13% added minorities.
  - 48% said they wanted women, but only 17% added women.
- **Expertise**
  - Financial: 55%
  - Risk: 24%
  - Regulatory/government: 20%

Women and Minorities
- **Nearly 90% of boards have at least one woman—a 3% change in the last ten years.**
- **Women account for 16% of all independent directors—no change since 2004.**
- **One-third of new female independent directors are current or former CEOs, etc.; 36% come from non-CEO corporate executive roles, versus 17% of their male peers.**
- **In companies led by women, 32% of directors are women, versus 15% at male-led firms.**

Trends
- **Few women are being added to boards: 17% of boards added women in 2009, a 6% drop over ten years.**
- **It has become more difficult to recruit sitting CEOs and top executives: 26% of boards were able to do so in 2009, a 51% drop over ten years.**

Source: 2009 Spencer Stuart Board Index

| Diversity and Governance

Spencer Stuart's statistics reveal a strong appetite for women and people of color (50% said they wanted to add minorities, and 48% said they were seeking women). The reasons for this are varied and are not mutually exclusive. Some companies face pressure from employees and shareholders for broader representation on their boards. Some might want the composition of the board to mirror the country's demographics or those of the desired consumer/customer base. Others see intrinsic value in diversity of thought that can lead to greater innovation and better governance and performance.

My own experience with companies attempting to recruit directors, especially minority and female candidates, was that often there was a gap between what the companies said they wanted and what they chose. The statistics above bear that out. So what is the problem? As a practical matter, there are relatively few female and minority CEOs, and while the number of division presidents and other senior executives who are women or people of color is increasing, it is increasing at a slower rate than it has in the past. One might suggest that companies seek a comparable level of expertise somewhere other than the corporate world. Indeed, nominating committees and executive search firms do troll the loftiest ranks of academia, the military, the government, and even the sports world to find accomplished and sometimes high-profile women and minorities. I can only conclude that the gap is attributable to unfamiliarity with underrepresented groups (women and minorities), resistance to change, bias, bigotry, or some combination thereof.

Diversity board searches are not limited to the United States. I worked on several searches where we sought women and people of color. We looked all over the world (and though it's redundant to say so in a book, I do mean that literally—we searched in many countries) for people with significant accomplishments in industries related to the company's core business and/or with relevant functional expertise (e.g., finance, risk management, etc.). There was considerable appeal to finding someone with knowledge of cultures and practices from other regions where the company in question might be operating or into which they were planning to expand operations.

In 2007 Norway enacted a law that forced the boards of publicly traded companies to be composed of no less than 40% women. Norwegian men and women alike expressed their resistance to the idea, saying it was reverse discrimination, that quotas are wrong because they negate the idea of a meritocracy, and even—get this one—women don't really want to serve on boards anyway. Well, two years later the general sentiment among Norwegian male and female directors is that boards were measurably improved as a result of the mandate and that the boards never would have changed without the legislation.

A 2010 *Wall Street Journal* article titled "Why Diversity Can Backfire on Company Boards," written by Jean-François Manzoni, Paul Strebel, and Jean-Louis Barsoux, suggests that the hoped-for benefits of board diversity can be elusive because of human nature. The article goes on to offer solutions for improving board dynamics in order to take advantage of diversity. At the end of the day, people's personalities, biases, and preferences dictate a board's composition and attendant interaction. History has shown that discord and dysfunction in corporate board rooms can cost shareholder value, so it is critically important to get the dynamic "right."

| Not-for-Profit (NFP) or Civic Boards

Most NFP organizations are by definition mission-driven and therefore don't have making money as a goal. They are service organizations providing programs, funding, or curricula to worthy individuals or groups; they are commonly known as charities, endowments, foundations, trusts, cooperatives, academic institutions, etc. Though profit is not the objective, NFPs do require financial and other resources to operate, and securing and deploying those resources in order to deliver on their mission takes a delicate balance every year, especially in light of shrinking funding pools. NFP board members or trustees provide input on strategic plans and policies, assist in the fundraising process, and act as visible advocates in the community. Your gratification, as a board member, comes from providing your time, money, and contacts to advance the mission of the organization.

Let's talk more specifically about what each of those three primary responsibilities really means. On a practical level, providing input on strategic plans and policies involves attending board and committee meetings and conference calls and offering an informed opinion based on your regular review of materials provided by the organization. Fundraising is critical, and you need to be prepared to share your personal and professional contacts in hopes of soliciting their financial support. Make no mistake, part of your appeal as a board member is based on how well-connected you are. Thoughtful nominating committees actively seek a wide range of professionals who represent increasingly diverse demographics (age, race, industry, function, etc.) to maximize their fund-raising base and possibly better represent their current or intended audience or program beneficiaries. It's not just about older, high-net-worth patrons and philanthropic corporate entities anymore.

As important as your contacts are, your own ability to meet minimum financial requirements is essential. Most NFP organizations have a "give or get" expectation, meaning they expect you to make a gift yourself and/or secure gifts from individuals or corporate entities in a given year. While you won't likely be summarily dismissed by the end of the year if you have done neither, you will, however, probably have a conversation with either the executive director or a member of the governance or development committee to remind you of your responsibilities. Your value or contribution can be demonstrated in other ways, such as facilitating alliances, securing in-kind or pro bono services, generating new ideas for programs or audience enhancement, and bringing a high level of favorable visibility to the organization.

This brings me to the last of the three most important responsibilities of an NFP board member or trustee: visible advocacy. Some not-for-profit boards are a "who's who" of a city's (or even a country's) business, social, political, and/or academic elite. Over time, an NFP organization might have amassed a coveted list of donors who give generously, influence other individuals and organizations to do the same, and lend credence and status to the organization's mission. In Chicago, the Art Institute, the Field Museum, and the Goodman Theater have high-powered boards and hot-ticket annual galas that "everybody who's anybody" can't wait to attend. Elsewhere, the Metropolitan Museum of Art, The J. Paul Getty Trust, Junior Achievement, and the Smithsonian Institution are but a few notable nonprofits that boast illustrious boards.

One does not ask to be considered for these boards; you really need to wait to be approached. The "give or get" number is high, as are the stakes for making an impression to establish, or maintain, your reputation as a hardworking and effective board member. Not all organizations seek the rich and well-known; most organizations want board members who take their mission to heart and are in the community talking about the merits of that mission and the strong rationale for supporting it. Similarly, not all would-be NFP board members are jockeying for the status that comes with serving on the largest and/or most prestigious organizations' boards. There are countless small and medium-size organizations in need of your expertise, commitment, and financial resources. Here are a few things to factor in when considering a not-for-profit board or trustee seat:

- **Let the mission move you.** I was enraptured by one of the Chicago Sinfonietta's performances, and when I was approached, I already had an appreciation for their innovative brand of classical music.
- **Know which unique skills you are bringing to the organization, and have an explicit discussion with the director or president, members of the nominating committee, and other trustees about their specific expectations for you.**
- **Get to know the other board members or trustees.** Determine if they are people you will enjoy working with and if you can benefit personally or professionally from knowing them.
- **Allocate time, and honor your commitment to attend board and committee meetings and events.**
- **Plan for the long haul.** Most boards expect you to serve for a number of years to fully benefit from your expertise, contacts, and other resources. If your circumstances change for personal

or professional reasons and you can no longer meet the requirements, graciously step down (before you are asked to do so).

Here is an overview of current trends and characteristics of not-for-profit boards reprinted with permission from the *Grant Thornton 2009 National Board Governance Survey for Not-for-Profit Organizations*:

GOVERNANCE

- "Nearly four in 10 (39%) of the organizations surveyed have between 16 and 30 board members, followed closely by boards composed of 6-15 board members (37%).
- **IRS Form 990 has caused NFP boards to focus on scrutinizing the performance of the board, CEO, CFO, and development director.** Three in 10 (30%) reported that one of the main ways the organizations' agendas changed in 2009 was that they spent more time evaluating CFO performance.
- **Similarly, Form 990 cast the spotlight on executive compensation.** Nearly three-quarters (73%) of respondents said their organizations have formal policies in place to review executive compensation.

TRAINING

- **Three-quarters (75%) of organizations held orientation sessions for new board members covering topics such as financial information, key organizational documents, etc.**
- **83% of survey respondents indicated that they read, understood, and interpreted the financial statements of the not-for-profit organization in order to exercise their responsibilities.**
- **Further training was believed to be beneficial in two areas: responding to issues raised within the financial statements (57%) and understanding the fundamentals of not-for-profit accounting and financial reporting (51%).**

ADVISORY BOARDS AND COUNCILS

Advisory boards are frequently assembled by privately-held companies, small business owners, or other non-public entities (such as academic or medical institutions) seeking advice and counsel from other business professionals from related fields or with specific functional expertise. Typically the senior executive will seek functional experts in marketing, accounting, and/or legal to be part of their advisory board to add perspective to the employees or vendors they have for those functions. The structure is far less formal than that of corporate boards, as there are usually no committees, just regular meetings for which the advisory board members may or may not be compensated. The benefit to the advisory board members is that they can share their expertise and be of service without express fiduciary responsibility or liability. They also get exposure to the ideas and perspectives of a new circle of professionals, which can be helpful in growing their own businesses.

Several large corporations have advisory boards as adjuncts to their larger corporate boards. They are often assembled to provide special insight into a certain demographic consumer base or particular event or topic of short-term interest or importance. Pepsi, as an example, has for years had advisory boards composed of notable African Americans and Hispanics to enhance their insight into those specific communities and ensure that their tastes, preferences, and values are being taken into consideration by Pepsi with regard to its products and initiatives. Colleges and universities often have advisory boards or councils of students, alumni, or other constituents as a structured way of gaining advice and support for programs and curricula.

Entry Level

You simply are not ready for a board seat yet, but you can gain exposure to not-for-profit organizations by volunteering and serving on committees, since you don't always have to be a board member to serve on a board committee. Many nonprofits welcome participation and input from younger people to maintain perspective on their audiences or other constituencies.

Mid-Level

Start getting active with a nonprofit or two to get experience and increase your visibility with other, more senior professionals. Only commit if you can make time. Give as much as is practical financially, but most importantly, develop a reputation for reliability and dedication to the organization's mission.

Executive Level

Now is the time when you might show up on the radar screen as a possible corporate board candidate. Be active, visible, and valued on civic and cultural boards you believe in, maintain an upward trajectory on the job, and you will be noticed in due time. Also consider raising your hand for advisory boards; effective networking can lead you to these opportunities.

Encore Level

You are most attractive by dint of your extensive expertise and accomplishments. Level/rank and function matter most to corporate boards, but don't be put off if you aren't getting the attention you want because you happen be in human resources, legal, or other staff functions; these functions are generally less desirable to corporate boards (see the statistics above). Seek out an advisory board that will appreciate your functional expertise.

Detour Route

Pedigree, rank, and tenure matter to corporate boards. If you are just getting (re-)established in a function or industry, give yourself some time before seeking a board seat, regardless of type. Get good at what you do, move up, make a lot of money, and then you can capture the attention of nominating committees.

13

CONCLUSION

Thank you for letting me be your guide on this journey. I hope that you will see the value in taking the free-agency approach to managing your career. You have chosen the path of introspection, discipline, and decisiveness by mapping, networking, and taking action to create opportunities for yourself. Remember that there is no single job that will fulfill all your dreams. Life and circumstances change at a rapid-fire pace. You now have a tool that you can turn to again and again as you chart your course in the new world of work. Revisit your career map at least annually.

On my website http://mycareermapping.com you will find a blank career map waiting for you to chart your course. You will also find my blog and lots of useful tools and information to help you along your way. Dig deep, reach out to your network, and take charge of your career and your life.

Here's to the adventure ahead!

14

ABOUT THE AUTHORS

Using the strategies and tools outlined in Career Mapping, Virginia "Ginny" Clarke realized that she was ready to make a bold move in her own career. In March 2009 she chose to leave her role as a partner and the leader of the global diversity practice at Spencer Stuart, one of the world's largest senior-level executive search firms. Committed to helping companies and individuals in these uncertain times she launched her business, providing talent management and career expertise. Through her firm, Talent Optimization Partners, LLC, Clarke provides corporate consulting and executive coaching services. She is a sought after speaker at professional gatherings, colleges and universities, and has been featured on numerous radio and television broadcasts.

During her 12-year tenure at Spencer Stuart, Clarke successfully recruited professionals in a variety of senior-level functions, including general management, finance, human resources, and marketing, as a member of the firm's financial services and financial officer practices. In her leadership of the diversity practice, Clarke worked with global clients to customize diversity recruitment and retention strategies. She also oversaw the firm's efforts to provide clients with diverse slates of candidates through knowledge management and by embedding diversity and inclusion into the firm's culture and infrastructure.

Prior to joining Spencer Stuart, Clarke spent several years in banking and 10 years in the real estate investment management business with Jones Lang LaSalle (formerly LaSalle Partners) and

Prudential Real Estate Investors. Her activities included asset management, portfolio management, capital raising, and client servicing. She received her bachelor of arts degree from the University of California, Davis in 1980 and served as a recruiter for the school after graduating. Clarke received her M.B.A. from the Kellogg School of Management at Northwestern University in 1984. In April 2009 she received a Kellogg Alumni Service Award. She serves on the boards of Medical Properties Trust in Birmingham, Alabama (NYSE: MPW) and the Chicago Sinfonietta, the nation's most diverse symphony orchestra. Mother to a teenage son, Julian, and married to Thomas McElroy II, California native Clarke is a longtime resident of Chicago.

Co-author Echo Montgomery Garrett is a journalist with 25 years' experience and author of several books, including most recently *Why Don't They Just Get a Job? One Couple's Mission to End Poverty in Their Community* (aha! Process, 2010) and *My Orange Duffel Bag: A Journey to Radical Change* (Operation Orange Media, 2010), which was the November 2010 book selection of the Pulpwood Queens, the largest book club in the nation. Her first book was the well-reviewed *How To Make a Buck and Still Be a Decent Human Being: A Week with Rick Rose at Dataflex* (HarperBusiness, 1993). She also ghostwrote *Tales from the Top: Ten Crucial Questions from the World's #1 Executive Coach* (Nelson Business, 2005). Her first business book received glowing write-ups in the *Wall Street Journal, Inc., Publisher's Weekly,* and several other publications on management issues. *Tales from the Top* was a summer read pick in the Harvard Business Review Online and was excerpted and well-reviewed in many publications for corporate leaders and human resource managers. After her selection from a field of 25 writers, Echo wrote *Dream No Little Dreams: How Clay Mathile transformed The Iams Company into the leader of the pack in the world of pet nutrition*, the authorized biography of Clayton L. Mathile, former CEO/chairman of The Iams Company.

Formerly an editor at *McCall's* and *Venture* magazines, and formerly a contributing writer for *Money, BusinessWeek, Management Review, Investor's Business Daily*, and *The Atlanta Business Chronicle*, Garrett has been published in more than 75 national magazines, newspapers, and websites, including *Parade, INC. Magazine, The New York Times, Delta Sky, Chief Executive, The Atlanta-Journal Constitution,* and Abcnews.com. She has been interviewed on Good Morning America, CNBC, CNN, and NY-1. She served as editor in chief of *Atlanta Woman* magazine. Her first issue took the gold for Best Single Issue out of 300 entrants at the 2005 GAMMA awards sponsored by the Magazine Association of the Southeast. The Auburn University graduate is a member of the Authors Guild, American Society of Journalists and Authors, Investigative Reporters and Editors, the National Federation of Press Women, Atlanta Press Club, the Buckhead Club, and the Buckhead Business Association 2009 Leadership Class. Married to professional photographer Kevin Garrett and mother to two sons, Echo is co-founder and president of the Orange Duffel Bag Foundation, a nonprofit that advocates for homeless youth and those aging out of foster care.

ATLAS

"TO TRAVEL HOPEFULLY IS A BETTER THING THAN TO ARRIVE."
~ ROBERT LOUIS STEVENSON

PHASE I   PLOTTING

INDUSTRIES SEGMENTS	I. TECHNOLOGY	II. COLLEGE ACADEMICS	III. EXTRACURRICULARS
FUNCTIONS *(e.g., finance, marketing, etc.)*	› Sales support › Lead generation › Marketing › Consultative sales	› Finance	› Sports › Music
FORMER ROLES *(Titles)*	› Inside Client Manager › Inside Business Partner Manager	› B.S. Finance	› IM Soccer › IM Softball › IM Flag Football › Radio show
COMPETENCIES	› Analytical › Marketing strategy › Consultative selling		

NEW INDUSTRIES	I. TECHNOLOGY	II. FINANCIAL SERVICES
NEW ROLES *(up to 3 per Industry)*	› Finance - Corporate finance - Corporate development/strategy - Risk management - Investor relations › Marketing	› Finance - Corporate finance - Corporate development/strategy - Risk management - Investor relations › Market analyst › Research associate/analyst
COMPETENCIES REQ'D	› Financial acumen › Analytical aptitude › Problem solving	› Financial acumen › Analytical aptitude › Problem solving
COMPETENCY GAPS	› Budgeting & forecasting › Capital utilization	› Budgeting & forecasting › Capital utilization
EXPERIENCE GAPS	› 3-5 yrs. in jr. role › International exp.	› 3-5 yrs. in jr. role › International exp. › Fraud bank/credit card payments › Book of business
PERSONAL ATTRIBUTES *(most useful, challenging or relevant to Industry)*	› Competitive › "Completionist" › Consultative	› Competitive › Analytical

Fictitious person, and all other personal information, including e-mail, addresses and phone numbers

PHASE I   PLOTTING

NEW INDUSTRIES	III. CONSULTING	IV. ENTERTAINMENT/SPORTS
NEW ROLES *(up to 3 per Industry)*	› Risk management › Research associate/analyst	› Finance - Corporate finance - Corporate development/strategy - Risk management - Investor relations › Marketing
COMPETENCIES REQ'D	› Analytical skills › Research capabilities › Organizational skills	› Financial acumen › Analytical aptitude › Problem solving
COMPETENCY GAPS	› (None)	› Budgeting & forecasting › Capital utilization
EXPERIENCE GAPS	› Consulting › Book of business	› 3-5 yrs. in jr. role › International exp.
PERSONAL ATTRIBUTES *(most useful, challenging or relevant to Industry)*	› Deliberative › Command › Adaptable	› Adaptable › Competitive

CAREER MAPPING
mycareermapping.com

PHASE II

TARGET COMPANIES

TECHNOLOGY COMPANIES	FINANCIAL SERVICES COMPANIES	CONSULTING COMPANIES	ENTERTAINMENT/SPORTS
HP	Merrill Lynch	KPMG	ESPN
Cisco	Bank of America	Accenture	Electronic Arts
Oracle	Wells Fargo/Wachovia	McKinsey	Ogilvy
SAP	Citigroup	Aon (Consulting)	Time Warner (Turner)
EMC	Credit Suisse	Deloitte	Nike*
Google	UBS	PWC	Adidas*
Microsoft (maybe)	Brown Brothers Harriman	Korn Ferry	NFL*
Apple*	Goldman Sachs	Spencer Stuart	PGA*
	Morgan Stanley	Russell Reynolds	USTA*
	JP Morgan Chase*	Heidrick & Struggles	Sony*
	Barclays*	Egon Zehnder	Disney*
	HSBC*		

Fictitious person, and all other personal information, including e-mail, addresses and phone numbers

PHASE III

NETWORKING GUIDE

NEED	CONTACTS	SPECIFIC QUESTION	ACTION STEPS
FINANCIAL ANALYST Informational interview	› Dan from Class of 2007	› Is it best to go through HR or someone in finance Dept.?	› NRB to introduce
MARKET ANALYST Informational interview	› Dad's old boss at bank	› What is typical entry-level background	› Ask Dad
RESEARCH ASSOCIATE Informational interview	› Sue's cousin at JPMC	› How similar are market analyst and research associates roles?	› Pick one idea or the other
MARKETING MANAGER Access to NFL	› Steve Whitfield	› Ask to keep in mind for opportunities	› Attempt to contact through LinkedIn

CAREER
MAPPING

PHASE I PLOTTING

INDUSTRIES/ SEGMENTS	I. REAL ESTATE DEVELOPMENT	II. CULINARY
FUNCTIONS *(e.g., finance, marketing, etc.)*	› Marketing -Outreach › Administration	› Product Development › Merchandising › Production › Training
FORMER ROLES *(Titles)*	› Marketing Manager	› Executive Pastry Chef › Pastry Chef › Asst. Pastry Chef
COMPETENCIES *(at least 4 for each)*	› Written & Oral Communication › Partnering › Continual Learning	› Creative Thinking › Problem- solving › Innovation › Continual Learning
INDUSTRIES/ SEGMENTS	III. ENTREPRENEURSHIP	IV. RETAIL
FUNCTIONS *(e.g., finance, marketing, etc.)*	› Product Development › Training › Management › Marketing › Sales	› Buying › Merchandising › Planning › Distribution › Training › Management
FORMER ROLES *(Titles)*	› Business Co-owner	› Fashion Buyer › Asst. Buyer › Sales Assoc.
COMPETENCIES *(at least 4 for each)*	› Problem-solving › Innovation › Creative Thinking	› Analyzing › Strategic Thinking › Leadership of small teams

PHASE I   PLOTTING

NEW INDUSTRIES	I. RETAIL	II. MUSEUMS
NEW ROLES *(up to 3 per Industry)*	› Merchandising/Buying › Visual Merchandising	› Event Planning
COMPETENCIES REQ'D	› Ability to interpret visual merchandising plan › Consumer trend analysis › Influencing/Negotiating	› Project management › Customer interface › Budgeting › Attention to detail
COMPETENCY GAPS	› Measurement, evaluation, reporting	› Budgeting
EXPERIENCE GAPS	› Product Development	› Media relations
FEARS	› Age › Lack of experience	› Age › Lack of Experience
PERSONAL ATTRIBUTES *(most useful, challenging or relevant to Industry)*	› Creative and artistic › Strong communication and listening abilities › Resilient › Somewhat introverted	› Sophisticated image and taste › Strong communication and listening abilities › Patient
AFFIRMATIONS	› I can pick and chose what I want to do	› New opportunities are opening up for me to use my creative skills and abilities

Fictitious person, and all other personal information, including e-mail, addresses and phone numbers

PHASE I

PLOTTING

NEW INDUSTRIES	III. HOSPITALITY	IV. PR AND MARKETING FIRMS
NEW ROLES *(up to 3 per Industry)*	› Marketing /Sales › Event Planning	› Event Planning
COMPETENCIES REQ'D	› Marketing/sales › Project management › Customer interface › Product / Service Management	› Project management › Customer/client interface › Business development
COMPETENCY GAPS	› Marketing/sales › Product / Service Management	› Budgeting › Client interface › Business development
EXPERIENCE GAPS	› Marketing › B2B Sales	› Media relations › Professional services environment
FEARS	› Age › Lack of experience	› Age › Lack of experience
PERSONAL ATTRIBUTES *(most useful, challenging or relevant to Industry)*	› Sophisticated image and taste › Communication skills › Resilient	› Sophisticated image and taste › Communication skills › Resilient
AFFIRMATIONS	› I can pick and chose what I want to do	› New opportunities are opening up for me to use my creative skills and abilities

CAREER MAPPING
mycareermapping.com

PHASE II

TARGET COMPANIES

RETAIL COMPANIES	MUSEUMS	HOSPITALITY COMPANIES	PR/COMMUNIC. COMPANIES
Williams Sonoma	The De Young	Kimpton	Charles Communications
The Gap Inc	The Legion of Honor	Joie De Vivre	Assoc, LLC (wines
Pottery Barn	S F MOMA	Union Square Hotels	and spirits)
West Elm	Museum of Craft and	The Huntington	Cross Marketing PR
BeBe	Folk Art	The Ritz-Carlton	(lifestyle)
Esprit de Corp	The Walt Disney Family		LCI – Landis
Wilkes Bashford	Museum		Communications
Haagen-Dazs			
Ciao Bella Gelato			

*Fictitious person, and all other personal information, including e-mail, addresses and phone numbers

PHASE III

NETWORKING GUIDE

NEED	CONTACTS	SPECIFIC QUESTION	ACTION STEPS
RETAIL COMPANIES Informational interview	> Joan has contact at Williams Sonoma	> Seeking role in visual merchandising	
MUSEUMS Informational interview	> Send résumé to Melanie > Contact through Phil		
HOSPITALITY COMPANIES Informational interview	> Kimpton > Sr. Dir. Communic.	> Who is best person to approach?	> Make 3 phone calls
Insight into current state of industry	> Bruce Harris at Joie de Vivre	> How viable are boutique hotels over large chains in this economy?	> Keep on list?
PR/COMMUNIC. COMPANIES Informational interview	> LCI is referral from Sue at SF Port	> Do people had longevity at City agencies?	> FU with Sue
Insight into current state of industry	> PR, Marketing > TBD	> Which firms are most successful/have best reputation?	> Contact 2 firms by April

ANTHONY R. CALLOWAY, JR.*

8 Pheasant Lane, Armonk, NY
Preferred: (914) 555-3901 | Other: (914) 555-2937 | arcjr@
aolgmail.com

SUMMARY

Seeking analyst-/associate-level opportunity in a sports or entertainment organization leveraging:

- Analytical Skills - Experienced in extracting relevant information from databases, as well as analyzing industry trends to support business development activities. Anticipate project needs effectively.
- Problem Solving Skills - Demonstrate resourcefulness and strategic decision making in proactively providing unique solutions to clients; accountable for solutions provided.
- Communication Skills - Excellent communicator, both written and orally; strong listening and presentation skills. Facile in both large and small group/team settings.

EXPERIENCE

INTERNATIONAL BUSINESS MACHINES CORPORATION, SMYRNA, GA | 2007–2010

Inside Business Partner Representative
January 2010–March 2010

Newly created role, focused on collaboration with IBM Business Partner channels and other third party resellers to create co-funded marketing campaigns and client events to increase revenue and profit. Group was disbanded due to changes in IBM business strategy, during company-wide layoffs.

- Created targeted lists for co-marketing call campaigns focused on industry-oriented solutions.
- Organized events to educate clients on IBM solutions and industry best practices.

Inside Client Manager
June 2007–December 2009

Provided consultative solution sales and support for a set of approximately 125 accounts, to internal and external clients. Concentrated industry focus on financial services and manufacturing and distribution sectors. Created and managed a network of IBM Business Partners and field resources to meet performance metrics.

- Established and implemented unique approaches in challenging market conditions.
- Exceeded 100% of revenue and profit quotas in 2007 and 2009; led territory industry peer group for attainment in 2008.
- Consistently ranked in Top 3 in department for call time and number of calls.
- Consistently exceeded targets set by Business Unit Executive for new opportunity identification.

*Fictitious person, and all other personal information, including e-mail, addresses and phone numbers

LEADERSHIP AND PROFESSIONAL DEVELOPMENT

- IBM Global Sales School Expert Mentor
  - Selected for leadership role focusing on practical sales skill building and training for new hires, 2008
- Dialexis SOAR (Surge of Accelerating Revenue) Selling System Training, 2008
- IBM Global Sales School, Graduated with Honors, 2007
- IBM ibm.com Sales Education/Training, 2007

EDUCATION

University of Southern California-Marshall School of Business, Los Angeles, CA

Bachelor of Science in Finance, August 2003-May 2007

- Trojan Radio - Co-host of "Bill & Kev's Excellent Adventure," a two-hour weekly radio show, 2004-2007.
- USC Intramural Sports - Soccer, flag football, softball, and basketball, 2003-2007.

RACHEL ANDERSEN*
5730 Peachtree Lane SE, Atlanta, GA 30082
Cell (770) 634--0893
Home (770) 430-9890
ryanders@yahoo.com

PROFILE
Strategic marketing executive with a strong record of results in marketing, manufacturing, and general management of consumer goods. History of strong collaboration and relationship building with diverse consumers, retailers, agencies, spokespeople and partners. Demonstrated ability to bring new and innovative approaches to both established brands and developing business models while leading multifunctional and global project teams. Consistently recognized as an innovative, passionate, and empowering leader with strong problem solving, critical thinking skills.

PROFESSIONAL EXPERIENCE
THE COCA-COLA COMPANY, ATLANTA, GEORGIA
2008-PRESENT

Assistant Vice President: Specialty Marketing
August 2008-present

Responsible for the start-up of marketing department following a ten year absence of company focus. Responsible for team of 7 with over $90 million in sales across all Coca-Cola brands (Coca-Cola, Sprite, Fanta, Dasani, POWERade, Minute Maid, etc).

Within first 6 months, conducted full portfolio business analysis to identify additional $20 million opportunity for future business growth. Developed targeted consumer and retail strategy including long-term objectives & goals, a financial model, and an organizational structure to capture upside.

Launched $10 million advertising campaign featured on the Super Bowl. Advertising created unprecedented positive calls to the 800-line and significantly increased all brand health measures by 10-50% (purchase intent, brand appeal, brand relevance, emotional connection, and believability).

Developed company's first Health & Wellness strategy. Led multifunctional team that secured celebrity spokespeople, coordinated national media and outreach, developed grassroots marketing programs, and placed media in key specialty outlets. Served as key spokesperson.

PROCTER & GAMBLE, CINCINNATI, OHIO
2000-2008

Associate Marketing Director: Marketing, Beauty & Household Needs
March 2006-August 2008

Developed strategic direction for corporate marketing efforts for all brands greater than $1B in sales: Pantene, Cover Girl, Olay, Crest, Always, Tampax, Tide, Gain, Pampers, Luvs, Bounty, Charmin, Downy, Folgers & Pringles.

Provided strategic leadership for $200 million budget, marketing plans, media, product initiatives, retail strategies, and measurement that resulted in a +3% increase in total corporate share.

Developed first P&G Beauty strategy to bring P&G's key beauty brands (Pantene, Cover Girl, and Olay) to consumers in a new way. Launched first Beauty magazine called "Total You" which doubled purchase intent of participating brands.

Fictitious person, and all other personal information, including e-mail, addresses and phone numbers

Brand Manager: Beauty, Herbal Essences and Infusium Brands
March 2004-February 2006

Led P&G integration of the two most profitable Clairol hair care brands during acquisition ($425 million in sales combined). Developed and executed short and long term strategic plans for the North America Herbal Essences business which accounted for 67% of worldwide sales.

Created $150 million consumer and trade promotion program. Increased Herbal Essences sales by 17% and Infusium sales by 18% within 6 months.

Defined unique Herbal Essences strategic positioning and identified highest opportunity target consumer segments that would maximize Herbal Essences share of the market and minimize cannibalization of other 10 brands in the P&G Hair Care portfolio.

Led multifunctional competitive strategy team to develop winning defense strategies for entire P&G Hair Care portfolio during highest ever levels of competitive activity.

Brand Manager: Multicultural Marketing, Beauty & Household Needs
June 2002-February 2004

Revived corporate effort to create winning African American and Hispanic marketing strategies. Became expert for company on "best in class" marketing plans and executions and trained entire organization.

Developed first ever corporate 5-year African American Business Plan that identified and defined strategies to deliver $300 million in incremental sales. Enrolled several key leadership teams and all senior management including CEO in the plan and led quarterly reviews with the CEO ongoing.

Assistant Brand Manager: Baby Care, Pampers Brand
August 2000-June 2002

Managed and executed against $100 million marketing budget and multi-channel strategy for making Pampers the first choice of new mothers.

Professional Endorsement: Negotiated $1 million contract with Dr. T. Berry Brazelton, world-renowned pediatrician, to be Pampers spokesperson for all newborn marketing efforts.

Advertising: Developed first ever Dr. Brazelton TV and print that ran in 50% of media weight.

Retail: Developed the first Baby Care shopper proposition that resulted in top tertile shopping conversion.

Internet: Developed first version of the Pampers Parenting Institute designed to educate and create a Pampers bond with parents. The site has undergone several expansions and is still in existence today.

Hospital: Developed plan to ensure Pampers was able to maintain consumer relevant claim of "used by more hospitals than any other brand."

EDUCATION

Masters of Business Administration, Finance: Columbia School of Business, EMBA Program - 2002 - 2006

Bachelor of Science, Mechanical Engineering and Material Science: Columbia University - 2000

PERSONAL, PROFESSIONAL AND COMMUNITY ACTIVITIES

Coca-Cola GLBT Forum: Vice-Chair - 2008 - present

American Advertising Federation (AAF): Mosaic Panelist - 2003

Washington D.C. Youth Mayor Award - 2002

DONALD BONAVIDES*
14 Elevated Road, Des Moines, IA 50396
Cell: (515) 555-3204
Home: (515) 555-6776
donbon@aolyahoo.com

CAREER OBJECTIVE

Corporate strategy and transactions executive with extensive change management experience seeking senior strategy or corporate development role in national health care services organization.

FUNCTIONAL EXPERTISE

CORPORATE FINANCE/TRANSACTIONS

Managed mergers and acquisitions, JVs, disposals, IPOs, and alliances; domestic acquisitions, disposals, and swaps. Led, structured, negotiated, executed complex merger and acquisition activity for identified, evaluated M&A opportunities.

STRATEGY/BUSINESS DEVELOPMENT

Led a team developing and executing business strategy and managing relationships with key partner companies for a multi-billion dollar division. Teams were across tax, accounting, treasury, legal, human resources, investor relations, public relations, risk management, financial analysis, marketing, and operations. Developed business cases and valuations.

PROCESS IMPROVEMENT/CHANGE MANAGEMENT

Reputation for building organizations, facilitating change, driving growth, reducing costs, improving core processes, and creating an inspired, high-performance culture. Collaborated with CEO, CFO, and Chief Strategy Officer of Citibank and members of the executive team to advance effective change management to ready the organization for new ventures.

PROFESSIONAL EXPERIENCE

BLUE CROSS BLUE SHIELD OF IOWA, DES MOINES, IA
(2005–PRESENT)

Vice President, New Ventures

Hired to lead investment activities to fuel the next stage of growth for the Blue Cross Blue Shield organization. Responsible for strategy, deal origination, analysis, project management, and business integration.

- Closed three transactions totaling $150 million resulting in a portfolio.
- Appointed to the Strategic Investment Advisory Committee of the Board of Directors of the venture capital fund sponsored by the Blue Cross Blue Shield Association.
- Conducted due diligence to support company's investment in venture capital fund sponsored by the Blue Cross Blue Shield Association.
- Recommended successful participation in two transactions.

---

*Fictitious person, and all other personal information, including e-mail, addresses and phone numbers

CAREER MAPPING
mycareermapping.com

CITIBANK, NEW YORK, NY
(2002–2004)

Senior Vice President, Market and Enterprise Growth Strategies

Developed strategy to aggressively grow top-line revenue for a range of new business opportunities that fully leveraged brand, business share, distribution, scale, and customer base, and delivered projected pretax potential of $250 million and $1 billion respectively for the Asian Customer Segment and the Customer Rewards and Loyalty Program. Led the corporate marketing Six Sigma initiative to develop an enterprise-wide Asian Segmentation Strategy.

- **Managing Director of Corporate Strategy and Development (2002–2004)** Led several key strategic initiatives, including divestiture of a finance subsidiary involving significant legal, regulatory, and operating risk and leading implementation of a new compliance infrastructure for a subsidiary.

VERIZON, INC., NEW YORK, NY
(1984–1999)

Corporate Director, Strategic Portfolio Investment & Management (1994–1999)

As the first Strategic Portfolio Investment Manager for direct equity investments, established investment principles and guidelines and monetized $300 million in the first year of operation.

- **Director of Strategy & Portfolio Management for the Internet and Networking Group within the International Networks Division (1990–1994)**, leading business development and strategic initiatives that increased top-line revenue growth and bottom-line earnings for the Internet and Networking Group by 15% and 10% respectively. Earlier roles in the International Networks Division included:
- **Director of Strategy and Business Development (1987–1990)** creating international alliances, licensing and marketing programs, and closing three transactions totaling $120 million.
- **Director, Business Development (1984–1987)** developing a vertical integration strategy to open new markets outside the United States.

LEHMAN BROTHERS, CHICAGO, IL
(1981–1984)

Investment Banking Associate

Responsible for client activity across all product lines and services for high net worth individuals and institutional clients. Took over territory of retiring banker. Secured nine new accounts in first year amounting to $36 million in assets.

EDUCATION

UNIVERSITY OF INDIANA
Masters in Business Administration (1981)
Concentration in Finance, Marketing, and Economics. Awarded a full two-year merit scholarship by Citibank.

NEW YORK UNIVERSITY
Bachelor of Science Degree in Physics (1979)
Studied in Rome, Italy. Work paper published in Science Today.

APPOINTMENTS AND AFFILIATIONS

- Member of the Board of Directors, Iowa Mental Health Association (2006–Present)
- Member of the Board of Directors, Broadband Concepts, Inc. (1998–2002)
- Appointed member of the Phillips Exeter Academy Alumni Council (1990–Present)
- Fluent in Spanish; reading knowledge of French. Enjoy golf, photography, drawing, traveling.

Fictitious person, and all other personal information, including e-mail, addresses and phone numbers

BUY A SHARE OF THE FUTURE IN YOUR COMMUNITY

These certificates make great holiday, graduation and birthday gifts that can be personalized with the recipient's name. The cost of one S.H.A.R.E. or one square foot is $54.17. The personalized certificate is suitable for framing and will state the number of shares purchased and the amount of each share, as well as the recipient's name. The home that you participate in "building" will last for many years and will continue to grow in value.

Here is a sample SHARE certificate:

THIS CERTIFIES THAT

YOUR NAME HERE

HAS INVESTED IN A HOME FOR A DESERVING FAMILY

1985-2010

TWENTY-FIVE YEARS OF BUILDING FUTURES
IN OUR COMMUNITY ONE HOME AT A TIME

1200 SQUARE FOOT HOUSE @ $65,000 = $54.17 PER SQUARE FOOT
This certificate represents a tax deductible donation. It has no cash value.

YES, I WOULD LIKE TO HELP!

I support the work that Habitat for Humanity does and I want to be part of the excitement! As a donor, I will receive periodic updates on your construction activities but, more importantly, I know my gift will help a family in our community realize the dream of homeownership. **I would like to SHARE in your efforts against substandard housing in my community!** *(Please print below)*

PLEASE SEND ME _____ SHARES at $54.17 EACH = $ $_____

In Honor Of: _____

Occasion: (Circle One)　　HOLIDAY　　BIRTHDAY　　ANNIVERSARY

　　　　OTHER: _____

Address of Recipient: _____

Gift From: _____　*Donor Address:* _____

Donor Email: _____

I AM ENCLOSING A CHECK FOR $ $_____ PAYABLE TO HABITAT FOR HUMANITY **OR** PLEASE CHARGE MY VISA OR MASTERCARD *(CIRCLE ONE)*

Card Number _____ Expiration Date: _____

Name as it appears on Credit Card _____ Charge Amount $ _____

Signature _____

Billing Address _____

Telephone # Day _____ Eve _____

PLEASE NOTE: Your contribution is tax-deductible to the fullest extent allowed by law.
Habitat for Humanity • P.O. Box 1443 • Newport News, VA 23601 • 757-596-5553
www.HelpHabitatforHumanity.org

CPSIA information can be obtained at www.ICGtesting.com
Printed in the USA
BVOW072328140113

310631BV00001B/106/P